Instructor's Manual to Accompany

Communicating Effectively:

Linking Thought and Expression

Third Edition

JOHN S. CAPUTO
HARRY C. HAZEL
COLLEEN McMAHON
DEANNA DANNELS

KENDALL/HUNT PUBLISHING COMPANY
4050 Westmark Drive   Dubuque, Iowa 52002

TABLE OF CONTENTS

PREFACE

This instructor's manual is designed to give teachers an overview of each chapter along with a series of activities and test questions to supplement the reading of the book.

As an instructor, you'll find a chapter synopsis followed by an outline. Both can be correlated with the cognitive maps found at the beginning of each chapter of the text. Any one of these items—or all three together—should give you the gist of each chapter. After the outline are teaching objectives followed by a set of two assignment categories addressed to students. The first category includes topics for journal entries or essays you may want to assign throughout the course. The second category contains in-class exercises. These are in addition to the exercises found throughout the book. Every chapter of the text includes some exercises designed to help students sharpen their communication and critical thinking skills, as well as help them consider the ethical and cultural implications of the subject matter. Some instructors find it helpful to have students write their reflections about interpersonal communication in an on-going journal. Such a journal can be used for students' private use or, at the discretion of both teacher and student, can be submitted in polished written form as a paper. The journal entries can be substitutes for essay assignments or they can be an addition to essays.

This manual also includes multiple-choice and true/false questions with the answer indicated by an asterisk. Following the multiple-choice and true/false questions are essay questions.

The authors hope this manual provides plenty of exercises, topics and exam questions for the entire course. Obviously, these items can be used in a variety of creative ways to make sure students are grasping the concepts and are able to apply them to their own lives.

Acknowledgments

We want to thank Kathleen Hazel who prepared much of the first edition of this instructor's manual. Special thanks also go to Anna Jo Baccellieri for her assistance in preparing some of the student activities in this manual. Donna Kincanon and Sandy Hank were extremely efficient and prompt in typing this booklet. The authors want to express their gratitude to all of them.

CHAPTER 1

INTERPERSONAL COMMUNICATION: A LIBERAL ART

CHAPTER SYNOPSIS

By developing their abilities to communicate, humans reach their "semiotic potential"—the unique capacity to create and understand meaning. Much of our time in growing up has been spent in building an effective **personal style**. For the most part, this process is informal and takes place through everyday experiences. Once we build a basic communication style, we grow only through a process of evaluation and modification.

Our personal communication style affects our ability to form interpersonal relationships. The importance of interpersonal communication to personal and professional success has been well documented. **Interpersonal communication** is an ever-changing transactional sharing that develops between people who are finding meaning with each other and come to know one another better as their relationship tends to move from impersonal to personal.

There are two basic views on what constitutes interpersonal communication: one is called the **situational view** and the other is the **developmental view**. The situational view deals more with the number of communicators while the developmental view focuses on the levels of knowledge communicators have of each other and the quality of their communication.

We communicate to meet interpersonal needs. Two motivational psychologists, Abraham Mazlow and William Shutz provide valuable insights for understanding how communication **motivates** us to meet our interpersonal needs.

Studying interpersonal communication from a liberal arts perspective helps students avoid a "cook book" recipe approach to improving their communication skills. Learning, from a liberal arts perspective, can only be the act of the learner and each must make informed choices about communication. The liberal arts approach also helps students realize that behavior with others often has ethical consequences. Because interpersonal communication engages us with other people, we can influence others in positive and negative ways. For this reason, ethics becomes important in interpersonal communication. **Ethical communicators** express the truth and avoid deception or manipulation in relationships.

To better understand and develop our interpersonal communication, we need to: gain self-knowledge; discover our commonality with others; understand the process of communication; learn to apply communication principles; recognize basic elements of communication; develop clear interpersonal ethics; and strive for quality in our communication.

CHAPTER OUTLINE

I. Developing Your Communication Potential
    A. Building Your Interpersonal Style
    B. What is Interpersonal Communication?
        1. Transactional Communication
        2. Shared Meaning
        3. Relationship Development
    C. Perspectives on interpersonal communication
        1. The Situational View
        2. The Developmental View

II. Why We Communicate?: Motivational Theory
    A. Abraham Maslow
    B. William Schutz

III. Why Take a Liberal Arts Perspective?

IV. Ethical Communication

V. Goals of This Book
    A. Gaining Self-Knowledge
    B. Discovering Commonality With Others
    C. Identifying the Processes of Communication
    D. Applying Communication Principles
    E. Recognizing Basic Elements of Communication
    F. Developing Clear Interpersonal Ethics
    G. Striving For Quality

TEACHING OBJECTIVES

▸   To emphasize the importance of interpersonal communication to personal and professional success.

▸   To present a definition of interpersonal style and how it develops throughout our lifetime.

▸   To describe with examples the difference between the situational and developmental views of interpersonal communication.

▸   To explain why a liberal arts, humanistic perspective can help make you a more effective communicator.

▸   To raise the question of ethics in interpersonal communication.

TOPICS FOR STUDENT JOURNAL ENTRIES OR ESSAY ASSIGNMENTS:

1.   After reading the definitions of interpersonal communication, reflect on several goals you would like to achieve in your own interpersonal relationships as you participate in this course.

2.   Think of all the people with whom you share a close, interpersonal relationship. Briefly identify 3 or 4 whom you'd like to share your experiences with as you continue taking this course and discovering more about interpersonal communication. How might this sharing enhance your relationship(s)?

3.   Remember as far back as you can into your childhood and write about as many influences on your interpersonal style as you can recall. Who were the key players? In what ways did they help shape your interpersonal style?

4.   Review Schutz's notion of our need for affection. How does this differ from our typical understanding of "affection." Think of ways that your family displays affection as described by Schutz.

IN-CLASS ACTIVITIES FOR STUDENTS:

1.   In small groups share your greatest fears and what intrigues you about participating in a class on interpersonal communication. Make a group list and evaluate the number of things you all may already have in common.

2.   Find a partner. With that partner, describe in as much detail as you feel comfortable, an interpersonal relationship that you currently would consider as being very important to you. Describe it from both a situational view and a developmental view.

3.   Using posterboard or a similar medium, do a collage illustrating Maslow's Hierarchy of Needs ladder. The key needs are: physiological, safety, love, esteem and self-actualization fulfillment.

Illustrations cut out of magazines or newspapers are effective. Share with the class.

4.   Watch a short film/video clip demonstrating dyadic communication. Then, as a class, discuss the elements of that form of interpersonal communication and whether all of those elements seemed to be employed in the clip. What made it a good exchange?

5.   Watch a film or video clip/scene (for example, "It's a Wonderful Life," with Mr. Potter confronting George Bailey in the bank scene) which demonstrates an unethical interpersonal communication pattern. What is happening in this sequence? What unethical elements are there? Why are unethical aspects being employed and to whose advantage? What is harmful about using unethical communication if it might be to my/your advantage?

6.   In small groups of 4 to 5, discuss how we all develop through our emotional connectedness to others and how we continue to need close relationships throughout our lives. (Re: Maslow's needs)

If we truly develop and "mature" as we grow older, why are such close relationships so important? Should they be so important? Does how we relate to every other person in our lives somehow tie in with our ability (or lack of it) to develop and maintain such close relationships? Discuss in some detail.

7.   As a class, discuss Albert Einstein's statement: "The uniqueness of man—the superiority of man in the world of animals—lies not in his ability to perceive ideas, but to perceive that he perceives."

Are most people perceptive? What does that mean? Do we learn to be perceptive over time or are we born with a degree of perception which stays fairly static throughout one's lifetime? Discuss.

TEST QUESTIONS

Multiple Choice

1.1   The following linguist developed the concept of "semiotic potential":

        a.   Aristotle
    * b.   M.A.K. Halliday
        c.   Bertrand Russell
        d.   David Berlo
        e.   George Simmel

1.2   "Semiotic potential" is the:

    * a.   unique ability to create and understand meaning.
        b.   the ability to share experience.
        c.   the ability to form strong, healthy relationships.
        d.   one's own interpersonal style of relating.
        e.   varied modes of communication.

1.3   Communication style:

    a.   develops through experience and observation.
    b.   continues throughout one's lifetime.
    c.   begins early in life with nonverbal messages.
    d.   is highly complex.
* e.   all of the above

1.4   The _____ style of communication is a set of learned communication values that we integrate with our personality, ethnicity, and cultural background.

    a.   cogent
    b.   interpersonal communication
* c.   personal
    d.   dyadic
    e.   motivational

1.5   Which of the phrases below best describes an ever-changing transactional sharing that develops between people who are finding meaning with each other and come to know one another better as their relationship tends to move from impersonal to personal?

    a.   personal style
    b.   transactional communication
    c.   dyadic communication
* d.   interpersonal communication
    e.   none of the above

1.6   Most linguists trace the humanistic study of communication as an art back to the time of:

* a.   Aristotle.
    b.   Martin Luther.
    c.   the Industrial Age.
    d.   the development of moveable type.
    e.   the 19th century.

1.7   The two major perspectives on what distinguishes interpersonal communication from other forms of communication are:

    a.   the personal and impersonal views.
* b.   the situational and developmental views.
    c.   the motivational and hierarchial views.
    d.   the psychological and sociological views.
    e.   the relational and theoretical views.

1.8   Communication factors such as the number of communicators and their physical
        nearness to one another are part of the _____ of interpersonal communication.

    * a.   situational view
      b.   developmental view
      c.   dyadic view
      d.   socialization view
      e.   none of the above

1.9   Communication between two people is most accurately termed:

      a.   dual communication.
      b.   transactional communication.
      c.   phatic communication.
    * d.   dyadic communication.
      e.   static communication.

1.10   The 19th century sociologist who first used the term "dyadic communication" was:

      a.   Edward T. Hall.
      b.   John Powell.
      c.   Kurt Lewin.
    * d.   Georg Simmel.
      e.   William Gudykurst.

1.11   Which of the following is not a characteristic of the situational view of interpersonal
        communication?

      a.   the number of communicators involved
      b.   the degree of physical proximity
    * c.   the social interaction patterns involved
      d.   the number of sensory channels potentially available for use
      e.   the immediacy of feedback

1.12   In the "transactional" model of communication:

      a.   each member of the communication process influences the other person.
      b.   each member of the communication process is being influenced simultaneously.
      c.   one moves from the interactional to the transactional perspective.
      d.   one shares some life-space overlap with every other human being.
    * e.   two or more of the above

1.13   _____ information relates to the individual's roles in various groups.

      a.   Phatic communication
      b.   Cultural information
  * c.   Sociological information
      d.   Psychological information
      e.   Qualitative information

1.14   DeVito claims that as relationships grow more interpersonal, the effectiveness of communication is characterized by:

      a.   positiveness.
      b.   openness.
      c.   supportiveness and empathy.
      d.   equality.
  * e.   all of the above

1.15   The best-known humanistic theory of motivation comes from:

      a.   Plato.
      b.   Machiavelli.
      c.   Gerald Miller.
  * d.   Abraham Maslow.
      e.   William Schutz.

1.16   According to Schutz's theory of needs, the three types of social needs satisfied through communication are:

  * a.   inclusion, control and affection.
      b.   openness, supportiveness and sympathy.
      c.   to love, to be loved and to convey love.
      d.   personal, intrapersonal and interpersonal.
      e.   formal, informal and relative.

1.17   A "liberal arts perspective" about interpersonal communication:

      a.   seeks to prepare a person to search for truth and thereby garner wisdom.
      b.   allows the individual to be free to learn or not to learn.
      c.   seeks truth through the unity of knowledge.
      d.   states that learning is an active process.
  * e.   two or more of the above

1.18   In describing "ethical communication," Johannesen states that:

    a.   ethical behavior is relative.
* b.   ethics is an important facet of interpersonal communication.
    c.   ethical behavior involves unconscious choices.
    d.   ethical communication is culturally inherent.
    e.   none of the above

1.19   The goal of recognizing basic communication elements is to:

    a.   keep life simple and predictable.
    b.   realize we all communicate the same way.
    c.   allow us to manipulate others.
* d.   clarify the similarities and differences among communication situations and relationships to see the basic elements of each.
    e.   strive for a universal language.

1.20   A fundamental goal of communication is to:

    a.   gain self-knowledge.
    b.   discover commonality with others.
    c.   identify and apply communication principles.
    d.   develop clear interpersonal ethics.
* e.   all of the above

1.21   Ethics in communication deals with:

* a.   what people may see as the gray areas of life.
    b.   deciding who is right and who is wrong.
    c.   making moral judgements.
    d.   the commonality of man.
    e.   none of the above

1.22   A basic assumption shared about communication is that it:

    a.   is static and unchanging.
    b.   is becoming more complicated all the time.
    c.   is worth working on because it can be improved.
    d.   provides quality of relationships as a by-product of quality communication.
* e.   two or more of the above

1.23   According to Schutz, _____ is caring and respect for others.

      a.   empathy
* b.   affection
      c.   love and marriage
      d.   discernment
      e.   phatic communication

1.24   _____ is feeling a sense of belonging.

      a.   Motivational theory
      b.   Affection
* c.   Inclusion
      d.   Intrusion
      e.   none of the above

1.25   Maslow's psychological needs include:

      a.   shelter.
      b.   food.
      c.   a clear perception of reality.
      d.   openness to experiences.
* e.   two or more of the above

True or False

1.1   Interpersonal experiences are the sharing of perceptions and meanings.

* a.   true
      b.   false

1.2   The ability to form strong, healthy relationships helps people develop competent selves which helps them take care of themselves and others.

* a.   true
      b.   false

1.3   The language skills developed during the first two years of life are among the most difficult learning skills mastered in a lifetime.

* a.   true
      b.   false

1.4   With our own personal communication style, we evaluate what we learn, choose alternatives and let other options go by the wayside.

    a.   true
* b.   false

1.5   Once you build your communication style, you grow only through the process of evaluation and modification.

* a.   true
    b.   false

1.6   Most scholars began to study interpersonal communication as a social science just after World War II.

* a.   true
    b.   false

1.7   Communication can be both unintentional and intentional.

* a.   true
    b.   false

1.8   Two people who communicate with each other find exactly the same meaning.

    a.   true
* b.   false

1.9   Meanings are in the receiver and are negotiated between speakers and listeners.

* a.   true
    b.   false

1.10   One way to distinguish interpersonal communication from other forms of communication is to consider the depth and quality of communication between communicators.

* a.   true
    b.   false

1.11   The terms "interpersonal" and "dyadic" are synonymous.

    a.   true
* b.   false

1.12   The developmental view of interpersonal communication ignores a crucial ingredient—quality.

      a.   true
* b.   false

1.13   "Life-space" is the totality or sum of learnings and experiences that make us unique.

* a.   true
      b.   false

1.14   In the developmental view of interpersonal communication, two people talking face-to-face are required.

      a.   true
* b.   false

1.15   In initial contact with others, we predict how they might respond to us given our first perceptions or impressions of them.

* a.   true
      b.   false

1.16   From the developmental perspective, all initial communication with another person is by necessity impersonal or nonpersonal.

* a.   true
      b.   false

1.17   William Gudykurst has found that all cultures try to reduce uncertainty during the initial stages of a relationship and do so in very similar ways.

      a.   true
* b.   false

1.18   Berger and Calbrese suggest that unfamiliarity with another person breeds uncertainty.

* a.   true
      b.   false

1.19   In "phatic communion," the words are somewhat irrelevant, but the social behavior is important.

        * a.   true
          b.   false

1.20   Generally, people base communication on cultural norms and social roles.

        * a.   true
          b.   false

1.21   As we continue to communicate with another person over time, our opportunities for gathering psychological information lessen.

          a.   true
        * b.   false

1.22   We only actively gather psychological information about another person when we choose to.

        * a.   true
          b.   false

1.23   In the "needs hierarchy," the highest need is the one for physiological fulfillment.

          a.   true
        * b.   false

1.24   According to the theory of hierarchial needs, if the needs are not met, or the needs are not met satisfactorily, people can become mentally ill.

        * a.   true
          b.   false

1.25   Psychologist Carl Rogers suggests that what one thinks is most personal to her or him, is often common with others.

        * a.   true
          b.   false

Short Essays

1.1   With one member of your immediate family (or with your boyfriend/girlfriend/spouse) how is interpersonal communication important in your everyday personal life? Expand in some detail.

1.2   How does interpersonal style develop?

1.3   Where would a homeless person likely be on Maslow's hierarchy of needs ladder? What task or tasks must a homeless person meet in order to progress up the ladder?

1.4   Why is discovering commonality with others an important goal of communication?

1.5   Bertrand Russell wrote: "Any definition is controversial and already embodies a philosophical attitude." How does this statement relate to interpersonal communication? Narrow your response to one focus—i.e. intercultural relationships, one-on-one relationships).

1.6   Where do you see yourself presently on Maslow's Hierarchy of Needs ladder?

1.7   How does the human social need to control get satisfied through communication? Provide a specific and detailed example.

1.8   What is your particular interpersonal communication style? Are you aware of having one? Do you understand how it has developed? Explain.

1.9   Cite one, specific, interpersonal experience which really had an impact on you. Explain the circumstances.

1.10   How is interpersonal communication a "liberal art?"

1.11   How can communication be intentional and unintentional? Explain in some depth.

CHAPTER 2

CRITICAL THINKING AND INTERPERSONAL COMMUNICATION

CHAPTER SYNOPSIS

In many interpersonal encounters, people often react with their hearts rather than their heads. Husbands, wives, children, friends, colleagues and strangers frequently respond on impulse without thinking through the consequences of their actions on themselves and others. As a result, virtually all people at one time or another, make choices they later regret. Critical thinking can help communicators make better decisions and thus enrich their relationships.

Critical thinking is the use of intelligent reasoning with supporting evidence used to make wise decisions. There are at least two benefits for practicing critical thinking in relationships. First, students can compare their communication patterns with what scholars maintain are effective ways to relate to others. Second, they can help themselves make decisions based more on sound reasoning rather than reactive behavior.

Critical thinking tools include syllogisms, enthymemes, evidence, and the ability to spot faulty reasoning. But since these tools relate only to the soundness of arguments rather than their truth, **cogency** can help people discover whether the arguments are also true. Howard Kahane describes cogency as reasoning that contains justified premises, relevant information and valid reasoning.

The use of the dialectic, reasoned criticism and the ability to detect fallacies of reasoning are also tools students can use to improve their communication. Besides fallacious reasoning, **prejudice** and **groupthink** can inhibit people from making sound choices in their interpersonal encounters. On the other hand, **reflective thinking** and **open-mindedness** to others can help produce more satisfying unions and greater harmony.

CHAPTER OUTLINE

I. Critical Thinking
    A. Advantages of Applying to Interpersonal Communication
        1. Scholarship
        2. Reflective Reasoning vs. Reactive Behavior
            a. Emotion vs. Reason

B. Tools of Critical Thinking
    1. Reasoning
        a. Syllogisms
        b. Faulty Reasoning
        c. Enthymemes
    2. Deductive and Inductive Reasoning
C. Cogency
    1. Evidence
        a. Facts
        b. Testimony
        c. Statistics

II. Ways of Using Critical Thinking
    A. The Dialectic
        1. Thesis, Antithesis, Synthesis
    B. Disagreement vs. Reasoned Criticism
    C. Fallacies
        1. Hasty Generalization
        2. Begging The Question
        3. Complex Question
        4. Ad Hominem
        5. False Analogy
        6. Slippery Slope

III. Conditions That Can Reduce Effective Critical Reasoning
    A. Prejudice
    B. Groupthink

IV. Conditions That Foster Critical Thinking
    A. Reflective Thinking
    B. Open-Mindedness

TEACHING OBJECTIVES

▸ To introduce the elements of critical reasoning.

▸ To emphasize the role of critical thinking skills in interpersonal relationships.

▸ To show students how fallacies can harm a relationship.

▸ To guide students in applying critical thinking skills to their relationships.

TOPICS FOR STUDENT JOURNAL ENTRIES OR ESSAY ASSIGNMENTS:

1.   Think of a time someone tried to persuade you to do something you did not want to do. What arguments did they use to persuade you? How did you refute these arguments? Critique the relevance and significance of the arguments and refutations.

2.   Think of an incidence where you fell prey to groupthink. What type of group were you in? How did this happen? How could it have been changed by reflective thinking?

3.   Think of a disagreement you have had with someone close to you. Did you argue from reason or emotion? How did emotion affect your reason? What role does emotion play in critical thinking and reasoning?

4.   Assess your critical thinking skills. How could you improve these skills? What are your strengths and weaknesses? How can an improvement in critical thinking skills better your interpersonal relationships?

IN-CLASS ACTIVITIES FOR STUDENTS:

1.   In groups of three, discuss a current issue having one person argue one side and the other the opposite side, with the third as a moderator. Have each person arguing think of 3-4 arguments and rebuttals to opposite arguments. The moderator is to supervise the arguments and rebuttals, watching for fallacies and cogent statements.

2.   Review Nixon's "Checkers" speech. What are the formal and informal fallacies in the speech? In small groups, discuss how these fallacies affect his ability to persuade.

3.   Write five examples of a "syllogism" for class sharing. Why is each syllogism valid or invalid?

4.   After viewing a clip from the movie "A Few Good Men" in which "reactive thinking" is evident, discuss in small groups how a reflective/critical reasoning approach would have had different consequences. (For example, you might examine Jack Nicholson's outburst toward the end of the courtroom scene.)

5.   Bring at least two examples of stories from the press that you believe to be biased or slanted. How are these examples of prejudice? What is/are the negative effect(s)?

6.   Bring an example of what "would appear to be" a "groupthink" process reported in a recent magazine or newspaper article. (i.e., a decision from a city council meeting, a committee formed to deal with a "hot" issue.) Be able to explain/defend how the "groupthink" phenomenon appears to be operating in this instance.

7.   For discussion: Do juries typically employ a particularly "groupthink"/"wolfpack" mentality, when it is a long, difficult jury trial and they all want to get it over with and go home? Is a juried trial truly a "fair" trial by one's peers then? How could/can the judicial system avoid such a pitfall? (The movie "Twelve Angry Men," staring Henry Fonda, is an excellent example of the above concept.)

TEST QUESTIONS

<u>Multiple Choice</u>

2.1   Critical thinking is:

      a.   thinking characterized by insistence on syllogisms.
* b.   the use of intelligent reasoning to help make wise decisions.
      c.   an insistence on deductive argumentation.
      d.   unambiguous statements of knowledge or belief.
      e.   negative thought.

2.2   The author of the <u>Phaedrus</u> is:

      a.   Aristotle.
      b.   Augustine.
      c.   Cicero.
* d.   Plato.
      e.   Darwin.

2.3   The syllogism is:

* a.   a three part statement containing a major premise, a minor premise and a conclusion.
      b.   an inductive statement.
      c.   a statement that is always logically valid.
      d.   a sentence in which the minor premise comes before the major premise.
      e.   none of the above
      f.   more than two of the above

2.4   An enthymene is:

      a.   an argument with evidence.
* b.   a syllogism with one of the premises missing, which also contains a probable conclusion.
      c.   the same as a syllogism.
      d.   a logical fallacy.
      e.   essential for interpersonal communication.

2.5   Which word or phrase below best describe the following statements: "All people who avoid fighting in a relationship are happy. Steve is somebody who avoids fighting so he must be happy."

      a.   enthymene
      b.   inductive reasoning
* c.   syllogism
      d.   fallacious reasoning
      e.   inductive thinking

2.6   Which word or phrase best describes the following statements: "Cheerleaders tend to be conceited. Megan is a cheerleader. Megan is conceited."

      a.   syllogism
      b.   faulty reasoning
      c.   inductive reasoning
      d.   deductive reasoning
* e.   two or more of the above

2.7   Which word or phrase best describes the following statements: "Terry is always punctual. Terry's bus ran late this morning. Terry was unavoidably late for class this morning."

      a.   enthymene
      b.   false analogy
* c.   inductive reasoning
      d.   deductive
      e.   syllogism

2.8   The dialectic is:

      a.   an important feature of cogency.
* b.   a method of dialogue in which a premise or hypothesis is continuously subjected to counter-argument.
      c.   an error in reasoning.
      d.   a deliberate form of fallacy.
      e.   none of the above

2.9   The dialectic is useful primarily because it:

      a.   allows for a clash of ideas.
      b.   often produces a solution that is logical and agreeable to both communicators.
      c.   generates new insights.
      d.   allows for the clarification of issues.
* e.   all of the above

2.10   A fallacy is:

      a.   a type of debate method.
      b.   a clash of ideas.
* c.   an error in reasoning.
      d.   a major kind of evidence.
      e.   a form of reflective thinking.

2.11   In the ad hominem, someone:

* a.   attacks a particular person rather than the issue under consideration.
      b.   draws a conclusion based on flimsy evidence.
      c.   argues in a circle.
      d.   makes an invalid comparison between two items.
      e.   forms a judgement before facts are known.

2.12   Prejudice is:

      a.   forming a judgement before facts are known.
      b.   a preconceived idea/notion which impairs critical thinking.
      c.   a negative, irrational opinion someone holds about a group or an object.
      d.   capable of fracturing interpersonal relationships.
* e.   all of the above

2.13   Groupthink is:

      a.   a thinktank.
* b.   strong pressure to conform to the majority opinion.
      c.   a method of reflective reasoning.
      d.   a form of critial thinking in a group.
      e.   an open-minded sharing of opinions.

2.14   The reflective thinking agenda was devised by:

      a.   Socrates.
      b.   Aristotle.
      c.   Plato.
* d.   John Dewey.
      e.   Irving Janis.

2.15   Open-mindedness is conducive to:

    * a.   critical thinking.
      b.   hasty generalization.
      c.   ad hominem.
      d.   false analogy.
      e.   groupthink mentality.

2.16   The dialectic method of dialogue was which person's chief teaching method?

    * a.   Socrates
      b.   John Dewey
      c.   Buddha
      d.   Aristotle
      e.   Richard Paul

2.17   In brainstorming:

      a.   each participant denounces other's ideas.
    * b.   each participant suggests ideas without stopping to consider if the suggestions
            will solve the problem.
      c.   individuals clash at the idea level.
      d.   participants seek easy solutions.
      e.   all of the above

2.18   A prejudicial person is one who:

      a.   is narrow-minded.
      b.   rejects ideas different from her own.
      c.   will exhibit intense attitudes.
      d.   won't even consider a viewpoint different from her own.
    * e.   all of the above

2.19   The first step in the reflective thinking process is to:

      a.   analyze the cause of the problem.
      b.   establish criteria for solving the problem.
      c.   reflect on the problem.
    * d.   clearly describe the problem.
      e.   seek a solution for the problem.

2.20   The tools of critical thinking involve:

    * a.   deductive and inductive reasoning methods.
      b.   reasoning and brainstorming.
      c.   the use of evidence and fallacies.
      d.   the use of emotion and reason.
      e.   disagreement and criticism.

True or False

2.1   In most interpersonal encounters, reflective reasoning is better than reactive behavior.

    * a.   true
      b.   false

2.2   You engage in reflective reasoning when you reveal early in a relationship as many points about yourself as you can.

      a.   true
    * b.   false

2.3   The syllogism must be both valid and true.

      a.   true
    * b.   false

2.4   Most people talk in enthymenes rather than syllogisms.

    * a.   true
      b.   false

2.5   The following is a deductive line of reasoning: "All football players enjoy competition." Sam is a football player and therefore he enjoys competition."

    * a.   true
      b.   false

2.6   It can be harmful to disclose too much about yourself too soon in a relationship.

    * a.   true
      b.   false

2.7   Most words are abstract and can have multiple meanings.

    * a.   true
      b.   false

2.8   The application of critical reasoning skills can solve all communication problems.

      a.   true
    * b.   false

2.9   Validity by itself does not guarantee truth.

    * a.   true
      b.   false

2.10   Reasoning is cogent only when it contains relevant information and valid facts.

      a.   true
    * b.   false

2.11   There are three major kinds of evidence: facts, expert testimony and analogy.

      a.   true
    * b.   false

2.12   Testimonial evidence refers to reliable witnesses or experts who can verify the validity of a claim.

    * a.   true
      b.   false

2.13   An expert is someone who can give credibility to a claim and make it appear more probable.

    * a.   true
      b.   false

2.14   In a dialectic, each communicator is open to the other's point of view and is willing to change her mind for the sake of learning.

    * a.   true
      b.   false

2.15   Fallacious reasoning is a form of cogent thinking.

     a.   true
* b.   false

2.16   Irving Janis coined the term "ad hominem."

     a.   true
* b.   false

2.17   Groupthink allows for individual differences but seeks a single solution.

     a.   true
* b.   false

2.18   The reflective thinking agenda establishes criteria for solving a problem.

* a.   true
     b.   false

2.19   Discovering causes is important because most problems have to be dealt with at the cause level to be solved.

* a.   true
     b.   false

2.20   The final step in reflective thinking involves each party brainstorming solutions.

     a.   true
* b.   false

Short Essays

2.1   With a specific example, please explain why reflective reasoning often produces a better relationship than reactive thinking.

2.2   Please explain how a knowledge of interpersonal communication theories and use of critical thinking can help improve a long-term interpersonal relationship.

2.3   What distinguishes deductive from inductive reasoning? Cite two interpersonal communication examples of each form of reasoning.

2.4   Define the dialectic method of critical thinking. Provide a specific example of how the method can promote interpersonal communication.

2.5 Using a recent media event, explain in some detail how either intelligent analysis or unthinking reaction brought about the chain of events and the final consequence.

2.6 Why is groupthink such a potentially dangerous mode of interpersonal communication? Please give two specific examples.

2.7 How does disagreement differ from reasoned criticism? Cite a specific example of each. Which method works better for fostering quality interpersonal relationships and then tell why.

CHAPTER 3

PERSON PERCEPTION

CHAPTER SYNOPSIS

Perception plays a key role in interpersonal relationships. Perception is an active process by which people assign meaning to experiences. This process involves the **selection**, **organization**, and **interpretation** of sensory data that helps people make sense of the world. Perceptual errors can cause problems in interpersonal relationships as people take action based on meanings they attach to particular situations.

A variety of factors can inhibit the accuracy of perceptions. **Intercultural** communication problems arise from varying perceptual interpretations of both language usage and nonverbal behaviors. **Implicit personality theory** is based on individual perceptual interpretations. One mode of impression formation is the **halo effect**, which implies that the first impression becomes the only impression to prevail. **Stereotyping** results from overgeneralizing or making weak generalizations about people, places, or events.

In addition to assessing others' personality traits, people often seek to project particular images of their own personalities. One way to do this is to display **identity cues**—particular styles of clothing or other nonverbal factors that give others a way to judge identity.

Misperceptions result from the nature of perception itself because perceptions are tentative, learned, and selective. Some additional barriers to perceptual accuracy are **allness**, **blindering**, **fact-inference confusion**, and making cultural assumptions.

People <u>can</u> work to increase the accuracy of their perceptions and decrease the chances for interpersonal misinterpretation and misunderstanding. Simply put, if people take more time and ask more questions before coming to conclusions, they can begin to improve their perceptual abilities. There are a variety of ways to seek more information. **Perception checking** and **empathizing with others** are two primary suggestions.

By understanding the perceptual process and making a concentrated effort toward increasing perceptual accuracy, people can increase their chances for more effective interpersonal relationships.

CHAPTER OUTLINE

I.   The Perception Process
    A.   Experience
        1.   Sensation and Perception
    B.   Perception
        1.   Selection
            a.   Selective Attention
        2.   Organization
        3.   Interpretation
            a.   Past Experience
            b.   Emotional State

II.   Perceptual Processes
    A.   Implicit Personality Theory
        1.   Halo Effect
        2.   Person Perception
        3.   Identity Cues
    B.   Stereotyping
        1.   Attribution

III. Barriers to Perceptual Accuracy
    A.   Allness
    B.   Blindering
    C.   Fact-Inference Confusion
    D.   Cultural Assumptions

IV.   Perceive Critically
    A.   Seek More Information
        1.   Perception Checking
            a.   Behavior Description
            b.   First Interpretation
            c.   Request for Clarification
    B.   Empathize With Others
        1.   Cognitive Level
        2.   Emotional Level

TEACHING OBJECTIVES

▸   To provide a basic understanding of perception and to emphasize the importance perception plays in interpersonal relationships.

▸   To present perceptual errors that contribute to weak interpersonal communication.

▸   To describe how guarding against perceptual errors can increase interpersonal effectiveness.

TOPICS FOR STUDENT JOURNAL ENTRIES OR ESSAY ASSIGNMENTS:

1.   A friend approaches you with this situation: one of her other friends perceives her in a particular way which is inconsistent with how she perceives herself. Your friend asks you what to do. What would you tell her? How would you help your friend deal with these conflicting perceptions? How would you handle a situation where someone perceives you differently than you are? How could you change these perceptions?

2.   Close your eyes and imagine yourself in a place where you feel very comfortable. This could be your bedroom, a favorite spot in your yard or a vacation spot; as long as you are completely comfortable in this environment. Imagine what you are doing. Watch yourself. How do you act and what are you doing? Visualize this private scene for a few minutes. Now, suddenly, you are aware that someone is watching you. How do you act differently? Does your perception of yourself change since you are now being watched? How do you view yourself differently when you know someone is watching you?

Continue this exercise by remembering a time when you thought you were completely alone but in fact, you realized someone was watching you. Write about the changing perception of yourself in this situation.

3.   Write about a time when you experienced selective perception. For example, on the first day of class did you perceive a professor by his or her reputation? If so, what was your selective perception? Did you perceive only the bad qualities of the professor since those were all you heard? Or, on a first date, have you sometimes perceived only the wonderful and romantic qualities of your partner? How did your perception change over time? Do you still maintain some selectivity in your perception of this person?

4.   Think of an important event in your life. Remember what you did (the facts), how you acted and what you felt. Talk to two other people who were involved in that event. Ask them to recall the facts, feelings and actions of you and the people involved. Compare the stories of the two others involved with your own reflection. How do these three stories compare? How does this illustrate the fact-inference discrepancy discussed in Chapter Three?

IN-CLASS ACTIVITIES FOR STUDENTS:

1.   Bring at least <u>one</u> visual example of the "figure-ground" concept. The example may come from a book, magazine, newspaper or other medium.

2.   Bring to class several large (perhaps poster size) pictures of non-famous, "every day" individuals in different modes of dress, hairstyle, expression, etc. After exhibiting each picture for a minute, have each class member write down a quick "first impression" sketch of each "personality." Compare first impressions. Are most of the first impressions similar or quite different?

3.   Bring <u>three</u> visual samples (pictures, posters, album covers, etc.) to demonstrate "identity cues."

4.   Watch the famous courtroom scene (1/2 hour) from "To Kill a Mockingbird." Is there an instance of "blindering" by the jury in this scene? Then in small groups, discuss how the jury failed to look logically and open-mindedly at the entire body of evidence.

5.   View a segment from the video "Still Killing Us Softly" regarding media stereotyping of women. In groups of three or four, discuss whether the speaker, Jean Kilbourne, provides through visual example, accurate or skewed examples of what she considers to be negative media stereotyping of women. Support your stance.

6.   Join with another class member and give a "first impression" speech. This speech should consist of the impression the speaker first had of the other class member. What did you infer from their initial observations? Reconstruct the person as you first perceived them.

7.   Small group discussion:
        What first impression do you think you make? Why do you think you make this first impression? Is your perception of your first impression consistent with what others in your group perceive? Do others in your group agree about your first impression? If not, how do they perceive your first impression?

TEST QUESTIONS

<u>Multiple Choice</u>

3.1   The process of perception involves the _____, _____, and _____ of sensory data that helps us make sense of our world.

    a.   sensation, experience, interpretation
    b.   sensation, distinction, limitation
    c.   differentiation, experience, limitation
* d.   selection, organization, interpretation
    e.   selection, distinction, sensation

3.2   Because we can only process a certain amount of what is going on about us at a given moment, we choose among stimuli and decide what we will pay attention to. This is known as:

    a.   a perceptual blinder.
* b.   selective perception.
    c.   a sensory experience.
    d.   a physical limitation.
    e.   attending.

3.3   Making a guess about what motivates a person and speculating that we know things about the person that we can't actually see is what Ross (1977) calls:

* a.   attributional biases.
    b.   first impressions.
    c.   false impressions.
    d.   making a judgement call.
    e.   overgeneralizing.

3.4   Which is <u>never</u> true about stereotyping?

    a.   Stereotyping can be far more harmful than helpful.
    b.   Stereotyping can help us determine how to behave in a particular environment.
* c.   More often than not, cultural stereotypes tend to be favorable.
    d.   Stereotyping results from overgeneralizing or making weak generalizations.
    e.   Stereotyping is a type of impression holding.

3.5   "I understand exactly how you must be feeling," is an example of the notion of:

       a.   sympathy.
   * b.   empathy.
       c.   paraphrasing.
       d.   perception checking.
       e.   allness.

3.6   The Gestalt theory of organizing stimuli holds that:

       a.   the perceptual process ends with selection.
   * b.   stimuli must be organized in some meaningful form.
       c.   stimuli cannot be meaningfully organized.
       d.   stimuli is largely subjective in perception and therefore cannot be organized or regarded with any validity.
       e.   all stimuli is abstract and must be discarded.

3.7   Interpretation is defined as:

       a.   selective attention.
       b.   a passive process in which people assign meaning to experience.
       c.   identifying specific stimuli to pay attention to.
   * d.   giving meaning to sensory data.
       e.   interpreting that which is normally abstract and incomprehensible.

3.8   First impressions are based on:

       a.   eye contact.
       b.   past experiences.
   * c.   physical characteristics and personal attributes.
       d.   what others think.
       e.   how we see ourselves.

3.9   The perceptual error that results from overgeneralizing or making weak generalizations about people, places, or events is:

       a.   selective attention.
       b.   first impressions.
   * c.   stereotyping.
       d.   first interpretation.
       e.   blindering.

3.10 A perceptual error that occurs when a particular characteristic profoundly influences all other impressions of a person is called:

* a.   the halo effect.
  b.   person perception.
  c.   stereotyping.
  d.   identity cue.
  e.   misperception.

3.11 Everyone makes observations of people's behavior and draws conclusions about other people's personality traits to predict how others will behave. This process is called:

  a.   identity cues.
  b.   halo effect.
  c.   stereotyping.
* d.   person perception.
  e.   fact-inference confusion.

3.12 A failure to distinguish between what one infers from a given situation from what is actually observed or known is called:

* a.   fact-inference confusion.
  b.   person perception.
  c.   allness.
  d.   blindering.
  e.   none of the above

3.13 A method of seeking more information to form a more accurate perception is to:

  a.   talk with the people you are forming impressions of.
  b.   describe the behavior you observe.
  c.   look for various possible interpretations.
  d.   seek clarification, if possible.
* e.   all of the above

3.14 When we feel sorry for someone we exhibit:

  a.   interpretation.
* b.   sympathy.
  c.   blindering.
  d.   empathy.
  e.   apathy.

3.15   Identity cues include:

    a.   particular styles of clothing.
    b.   decoration of office.
    c.   the use of jewelry or hair style.
    d.   posture or gesture.
* e.   all of the above

3.16   If someone makes a judgement about us that is not consistent with what we believe about ourselves, we tend to screen out that information, thus creating and reinforcing the notion of:

    a.   blindering.
    b.   halo effect.
    c.   stereotyping.
* d.   an illusory self-concept.
    e.   first impression.

3.17   Stereotyping can help us to determine how to behave in a particular environment by:

* a.   providing behavioral expectations.
    b.   categorizing people according to cultural background.
    c.   responding to people's rules.
    d.   responding to people's occupations.
    e.   predicting character.

3.18   Which of the following statements is not true regarding the use of facts?

    a.   facts may be made only after observation or experience
    b.   facts are limited to what has been observed
* c.   facts represent varying degrees of probability
    d.   facts can be offered by the observer only
    e.   facts refer to the past or to the present

3.19   Which of the following statements regarding the "figure-ground" concept is not true?

    a.   we make sense of stimuli by noticing either the figure or the ground
    b.   the labeling of an object and its background
    c.   we organize in terms of figure and ground
* d.   it is solely a black and white concept
    e.   three-dimensional cues are not necessary

3.20   Which of the following statements is <u>not true</u> about the concept of interpretation?

        a.   past experience plays a key role
     * b.   interpretation is largely intuitive
        c.   interpretation gives meaning
        d.   interpretation is influenced by one's emotional state
        e.   interpretation is often based on false assumptions

<u>True or False</u>

3.1   Past experience plays a key role in our interpretation of situations.

     * a.   true
        b.   false

3.2   First impressions are generally quite accurate.

        a.   true
     * b.   false

3.3   The halo effect is the direct result of stereotyping.

        a.   true
     * b.   false

3.4   The first step in perception checking is to describe what you are observing.

     * a.   true
        b.   false

3.5   Perceptual interpretations are generally tentative and subject to change.

     * a.   true
        b.   false

3.6   People exercise some control over what they perceive.

     * a.   true
        b.   false

3.7   What motivates a person today in her perceptual selection will necessarily motivate
       her in the future.

       a.   true
    * b.   false

3.8   People are limited by both psychological and physiological factors.

    * a.   true
       b.   false

3.9   As information taken in becomes more ambiguous, the chances for perceptual errors
       increase.

    * a.   true
       b.   false

3.10   The interpretation step in perception can be influenced by one's emotional state.

    * a.   true
       b.   false

3.11   Intercultural communication problems arise from varying perceptual interpretations of
       both language usage and nonverbal behaviors.

    * a.   true
       b.   false

3.12   Rarely do gestures lead to communication problems.

       a.   true
    * b.   false

3.13   Eye contact is culturally specific.

    * a.   true
       b.   false

3.14   Generally, stereotyping can be far more helpful than harmful.

       a.   true
    * b.   false

3.15   As a rule, the more we are able to discriminate <u>among</u> individuals, the less we will actively discriminate <u>against</u> individuals."

    * a.   true
       b.   false

3.16   For the most part, people base perceptions on accurate data collection and observable behavior.

       a.   true
    * b.   false

3.17   People often seek to project particular images of their own personalities.

    * a.   true
       b.   false

3.18   People tend to consider what they perceive or view in a given situation as reality.

    * a.   true
       b.   false

3.19   Some people are better than others at making accurate perceptual judgements and interpretations of others.

    * a.   true
       b.   false

3.20   People fall victim to "allness" when they open themselves to new or different information.

       a.   true
    * b.   false

Short Essays

3.1   Define the following terms and explain how they function as perceptual filters:

     a.   allness
     b.   blindering
     c.   fact-inference confusion

3.2   Discuss two of the many factors that can inhibit the accuracy of our perceptions. Then, suggest ways to avoid these perceptual errors.

3.3   Discuss two examples of age-discrimination stereotyping. Why is such stereotyping unfair and potentially harmful? Be specific as it relates to these two examples.

3.4   Discuss how "empathy" can be a more positive response than "sympathy" in a particular situation. How might sympathy alone be counter-productive to effective interpersonal communication?

3.5   Cite an incidence in your recent past when the "halo effect" prevailed. What were the circumstances? How did the situation resolve itself? Be specific.

3.6   Do men tend to use certain key identity cues? Do women use similar or markedly different identity cues? Be detailed enough to support your answers.

3.7   Discuss, by an example, how a particular inference was made that was not based on fact. How was the situation corrected?

3.8   Elaborate on an instance in which your first impression of someone proved to be "way off." What traits did the person seem to possess which contributed to the largely inaccurate first impression? What did you learn from this experience?

3.9   How does one's emotional state at a given time influence one's perceptual interpretation? What measures can be taken to insure that emotionalism doesn't cloud judgement or perception?

3.10   What is meant by "selective attention?" How can this be a problem in the workplace? In a committee meeting? What steps can be taken to avoid this pitfall? (Remember, we consciously and unconsciously select perceptive stimuli in order to filter out a bombardment of stimuli at any given time.)

CHAPTER 4

THE SELF-CONCEPT AND INTERPERSONAL COMMUNICATION

CHAPTER SYNOPSIS

The relationship we have with ourself is the longest and, in one sense, the most important we will ever have. The self-concept—strong, weak or somewhere in between—affects interactions with others. Therefore it is a crucial component of interpersonal communication.

The self-concept is the subjective collection of one's attitudes and beliefs built up over a lifetime. The development of the self-concept takes place in discernible stages known as **personification** and **role-playing** both real and symbolic. The self-concept continues to be sculpted by the relationships and messages people receive, especially from significant others. This accumulation of messages helps create what Wilmot calls a "residual self"—or remembered past experiences. Such past experiences impact how people relate to others. This, in turn, can influence how they can **self-monitor**. A high self-monitor is someone who can read a situation and then adapt to whatever the situation requires. A low self-monitor presents the same self, no matter what the circumstances.

The self-concept is multi-faceted: people feel confident about themselves in some areas but not in others. Self-perception helps explain the **self-fulfilling prophecy**—the notion that how people perceive themselves often determines the way they act. Thus, a job applicant who believes he will stumble during the interview could bring about the very action he fears because of his attitude.

Most people continue to take at face value comments others make about them. This **reflected appraisal** influences their interactions with others. Critical thinking can help sort out the valid from the invalid in messages others give us. Supportive language both from self and others can help bolster the self-image.

Four specific ways to strengthen a self-concept are: **reflection**, **vivid imagery**, **constructive self-talk** and a healthy **sense of humor**. These are especially useful when practiced together and reinforced until they become habitual.

CHAPTER OUTLINE

I.   The Self-Concept
        A.   Self-Esteem
        B.   Self-Image Development: Stages
        C.   Residual Self-Concept
                1.   Self-Monitors
                2.   High and Low Self-Monitors
        D.   Multi-Faceted Self-Concept
        E.   Self-Fulfilling Prophecy

II.   The Self-Concept and Communication With Others
        A.   Reflected Appraisal
        B.   Raising Self-Esteem Through Supportive Language

III.   Ways of Strengthening the Self-Concept
        A.   Reflection
        B.   Vivid Imagery
        C.   Constructive Self-Talk

D.   Sense of Humor
E.   Power of Habit

TEACHING OBJECTIVES

▸   To discuss the role of self-concepts in interpersonal communication.

▸   To explain how self-concepts develop and affect our interpersonal relationships.

▸   To explore methods for strengthening the self concept.

TOPICS FOR STUDENT JOURNAL ENTRIES OR ESSAY ASSIGNMENTS:

1.   Complete the following sentences:

-I wish...
-I dream of...
-I love...
-I dislike...
-When I have a problem...
-I am afraid of...
-My goal is...
-When I do something wrong...
-My family...
-My best quality...
-I value...

Choose two of your responses and write a brief paragraph explaining how your answers reveal your concept of yourself.

2.   Review the section in the text on self-fulfilling prophecies. Recall an example from your life of a self-fulfilling prophecy. For example, you tell yourself you are clumsy around men, especially on a first date. You tell yourself this so much that when you go on a first date you are clumsy. Your thoughts shape your behavior. Or you believe you are competent and intelligent entering a job on the first day and, in fact, you find yourself acting competent and intelligent. Think of an example of either a positive or negative self-fulfilling prophecy. Explain how your thoughts and beliefs shaped your behavior.

3.   Write a paper on the topic: "Who Am I?"

4.   Self image refers to how you view yourself while self-esteem is how you feel about that view of yourself. Write about one aspect of your self-image and self-esteem. For example, one area where self-image and self-esteem come into play is with academics. Others might

include your physical attributes, your social self, or your emotional self. Choose one and write about how you view yourself and how you feel about that image.

IN-CLASS ACTIVITIES FOR STUDENTS:

1. Materials needed: Butcher paper and crayons. Draw pictures of the ten most important events in their life which has shaped who they are now. Then draw the ten events on butcher paper, an event in one square until there are 10 squares. The paper will conclude as a story of framing the "self." Explain each drawing, telling about the events and how they shaped you into who you are now.

2. Think of 5-10 words which describe yourself. For example: responsible, slow-moving, simple-minded, kind, or exciting. Pair up and discuss why you believe each word describes you and give each other feedback on the accuracy of your self-concept.

3. Bring an album, photo collàge or scrapbook with no more than 10 photos that, in your own view, sums up how you "see" yourself. You need to display with your "visual self-image collection" a one-page, typed summary of your self-image. Share with everyone else in the class.

4. Bring one visual example to demonstrate the concepts of "personification," "imitation" and/or "role-playing." Photos, magazine or newspaper photos, postcards, or other media may be used.

5. Bring at least two visual examples of "role reversal." "Role reversal" is where a boy or girl, man or woman, assumes a role or task generally assigned to the other gender in that culture.

6. In her book, <u>The Dance of Intimacy</u>, author Harriet Goldhor Lerner states that "people need us to be a certain way <u>for their own sake</u>, and for the most complex variety of unconscious reasons. Throughout our lives, we learn that the survival of our relationships, and the very integrity of our family depend on our being this way or that."

Using the concept of the "residual self," write a 1-2 page statement of how your present self-image has been molded by your family's expectations.

7. List 5 things you strongly like about yourself and why. List 5 things you dislike about yourself and why those traits are distasteful. List any steps you might take to further strengthen the positive traits and to curb the negative traits.

TEST QUESTIONS

Multiple Choice

4.1   A healthy self-concept is important in interpersonal communication because:

      a.   someone with a strong self-concept is normally better equipped to deal with difficulties.
      b.   two people with strong self-concepts usually have a better interpersonal relationship than those who don't.
      c.   a positive self-concept helps us accurately perceive the outside world.
      d.   none of the above
* e.   more than one of the above

4.2   Self-concept is:

      a.   how intelligent you believe you are.
* b.   the subjective collection of all your attitudes and beliefs built up through your entire life.
      c.   the way others perceive you.
      d.   self-centeredness.
      e.   the ability to look at yourself positively.

4.3   The person who theorized that the human central nervous system is like a computer was:

      a.   Allen Monroe.
      b.   Wesley Baxter.
      c.   Albert Einstein.
      d.   Marie Johnson.
* e.   Norbert Wiener.

4.4   According to Sullivan, a child has a "wrong experience" when:

* a.   a child has a need and the need is not met.
      b.   the need is met, but the child still experiences tension.
      c.   the experience comes too early in a child's life.
      d.   the experience negatively affects the self-concept.
      e.   none of the above

4.5   At around seven months, a child makes a distinction between herself and her mother or mother figure. This is known as:

        a.   imitation.
        b.   role playing.
        c.   symbolic role playing.
    * d.   personification.
        e.   more than two of the above

4.6   In looking inward to self, how well you like what you see is termed:

        a.   self-concept.
    * b.   self-esteem.
        c.   personification.
        d.   self-fulfilling prophecy.
        e.   reflected appraisal.

4.7   The psychologist who pointed out that at birth a child sees him or herself only as an extension of the mother or a mother substitute was:

        a.   Norbert Weiner.
    * b.   Harry Stack Sullivan.
        c.   George Herbert Mead.
        d.   William Wilmot.
        e.   none of the above

4.8   Which of the following statements is not true about the human mind?

    * a.   the human mind is capable of storing an infinite amount of information
        b.   the human mind absorbs information from outside itself
        c.   the human mind stores information in the memory section of the brain
        d.   the brain houses billions of human circuits called neurons with their dendrites, synapses and cell bodies
        e.   the human mind is much more complicated than the most sophisticated word processor

4.9   Which of the following terms is not one of the four stages in developing personal identity and shaping the self-image?

        a.   personification
        b.   imitation
        c.   role-playing
    * d.   self-monitoring
        e.   symbolic role-playing

4.10   The crucial stage in the development of self-identity in which the self separates from the mother is known as:

      a.   initiation of the self.
      b.   the separation stage.
  * c.   personification.
      d.   role dismemberment.
      e.   self-concept stage.

4.11   The stage in self-image development in which the child mimics the actions of others, but without realizing why is known as the:

  * a.   imitation stage.
      b.   role-playing stage.
      c.   symbolic role-playing stage.
      d.   reflected appraisal stage.
      e.   none of the above.

4.12   Which of the following statements is not true about the self-concept?

      a.   Self-concept can be divided into categories such as social, moral, intellectual and physical.
      b.   Everyone has a sense of social self.
  * c.   Most people have low self-esteem.
      d.   Few people like everything about themselves.
      e.   Some people have strong self-concepts.

4.13   The notion that how you think about yourself often shapes how you'll act in certain situations is described as:

      a.   role-playing.
  * b.   the self-fulfilling prophecy.
      c.   residual self-concept.
      d.   self-monitor.
      e.   personification.

4.14   According to Missildines's theory of the "inner child of the past,"

      a.   the past is essentially an insignificant factor in the self-concept.
      b.   the child in us is left behind once we enter the adolescent stage of development.
      c.   only two people enter the marriage bed.
  * d.   the "inner child" still lingers in the memory of the adult and continues to influence the adult's behavior.
      e.   each of the two marriage partners enter the marriage bed with their childhood pasts behind them.

4.15   The concept whereby people define themselves in terms of what others have said about them is called:

        a.   role-playing.
        b.   symbolic role-playing.
        c.   self-fulfilling prophecy.
        d.   self-monitor.
  * e.   reflected appraisal.

4.16   One of the following is not a technique for strengthening self-concept:

  * a.   role reversal
        b.   reflection
        c.   vivid imagery
        d.   constructive self-talk
        e.   maintaining a sense of humor about oneself

4.17   In "vivid imagery" we:

        a.   repeat positive comments to ourselves.
        b.   focus on our past successes.
  * c.   use the imagination to see a scene before it occurs.
        d.   examine vivid language.
        e.   all of the above

4.18   People with high self-esteem:

        a.   like the way they are.
        b.   don't dwell on their liabilities.
        c.   focus on their strengths.
        d.   don't put others down.
  * e.   all of the above

4.19   To maintain a healthy self-concept:

  * a.   focusing is crucial.
        b.   be self-critical and downplay positive attributes.
        c.   develop a superior attitude.
        d.   pay attention to the flaws in others.
        e.   don't allow any criticism of yourself.

4.20   The person who developed the "residual self-concept" theory is:

        a.   George Herbert Mead.
    *   b.   William Wilmot.
        c.   Freud.
        d.   Clarence Missildine.
        e.   Horace Mann.

True or False

4.1   Self-concept and self-esteem are exactly the same.

        a.   true
    *   b.   false

4.2   The self-concept is shaped by the relationships we have with significant other people.

    *   a.   true
        b.   false

4.3   In "symbolic role-playing," a child must actually play the role in real life rather than in his mind.

        a.   true
    *   b.   false

4.4   The "residual self" is the lingering self-image produced by years of conditioning from significant other people.

    *   a.   true
        b.   false

4.5   A high "self-monitor" is someone who can read a situation accurately and then act according to that reading.

    *   a.   true
        b.   false

4.6   In one sense, the longest and most important relationship you'll ever have is the one you have with yourself.

    *   a.   true
        b.   false

4.7   A problem can occur when high self monitors never step out of the roles they want to play, thereby robbing others of seeing them as they really are most of the time.

    * a.   true
      b.   false

4.8   The feedback you receive from others is not vital to the formation of self-concept.

      a.   true
    * b.   false

4.9   If infants get negative or mixed messages, they start developing a poor self-image.

    * a.   true
      b.   false

4.10   A positive or negative self-image is something you're born with.

      a.   true
    * b.   false

4.11   In a "bad experience," a child has a need satisfied but still detects from the mother a feeling of tension.

    * a.   true
      b.   false

4.12   People who have gone through a number of "bad" or "wrong" experiences are not really impacted by these experiences.

      a.   true
    * b.   false

4.13   In "role-playing," a child has some idea she is playing a role.

    * a.   true
      b.   false

4.14   Roles, according to George Herbert Mead, are not important in shaping the self-concept.

      a.   true
    * b.   false

4.15   How we view ourselves has a lot to do with how we relate to others.

* a.   true
b.   false

4.16   According to Martha Washington, the greater part of our happiness or misery depends on our dispositions and not on our circumstances.

* a.   true
b.   false

4.17   The use of "reflection" can help us rehearse difficult situations in advance.

a.   true
* b.   false

4.18   Discipline is important in re-sculpting the self-concept.

* a.   true
b.   false

4.19   A change of habit works best when we are flexible and laid back about any changes we wish to make.

a.   true
* b.   false

4.20   A healthier self-concept allows us to feel better about ourselves, thus enhancing our ability to develop better interpersonal relationships.

* a.   true
b.   false

Short Essays

4.1   Please describe how a negative self-concept can influence a relationship between two people.

4.2   Joe is a low "self-monitor" who is preparing for an important job interview after graduation from college. Please demonstrate how his role as a low self monitor could impact positively or negatively the outcome of the interview.

4.3   Discuss how the relationship with the self is, in fact, the most significant of all relationships we'll have in our lifetime.

4.4   Use a personal example of "residual self" to describe how your self-image has been a product of years of conditioning from your parents, peers or "significant others."

4.5   How is the self-concept multi-faceted? Please provide specific examples from your own self-concept or of someone you know.

4.6   How is the self-concept tied in to the "self-fulfilling prophecy?" How have you reacted in a specific situation where you allowed a "self-fulfilling prophecy" to take over?

4.7   Describe how a sense of humor raised your self-esteem and allowed for improved interpersonal communication.

4.8   How does "habit" play a role in the strengthening of the self-concept? Has it worked for you? Explain.

4.9   Provide three personal examples of how your self-esteem was raised by supportive language. What were the circumstances in each of the three instances?

4.10   How does a sense of humor allow us to build rapport with others? Allow for a one-page response.

CHAPTER 5

MODELS OF RELATIONAL DEVELOPMENT: FROM INITIAL MEETINGS TO BECOMING MORE INTIMATE

CHAPTER SYNOPSIS

For better or for worse, when someone meets someone else for the first time, both develop impressions of each other that influence the chances of this relationship growing—or not. In conversations with new acquaintances, people generally talk about superficial information such as the weather, sports, or some factual, non-opinionated material. Interpersonal relationships develop by moving through this phase of **small talk**.

Part of one's interpersonal style has to do with gathering information about others. Two particular approaches useful in developing relationships are **self-disclosure** and **rhetorical sensitivity**. Self-knowledge or self-awareness is helpful in self-disclosure because what you choose to share with others is your true understanding of self. To increase self-awareness, it may be helpful to look at the **Johari Window** model which attempts to illustrate there are things one knows and things one doesn't know about his/her self as well as things that others know or don't know about the individual.

Another model of self-disclosure is known as the **Social Penetration** model which depicts disclosure as a gradual developmental process.

An alternative concept to that of self-disclosure in relationships and gaining knowledge of other people is **"rhetorical sensitivity."** This approach requires an adaptive approach to others that balances one person's self-interests with the interests of others.

Because a relationship implies an **interdependence**, each person needs to feel a sense of personhood. That is, each matters, each can influence and be influenced by the other and can help each other. The types of responses people give each other give them confirmation or disconfirmation. **Confirming** and **disconfirming responses** are communicated by a combination of verbal and nonverbal behaviors.

Lastly, regardless of one's understanding of communication context and goals, an interpersonal relationship will not grow and develop unless both parties are receptive and responsive to each other.

CHAPTER OUTLINE

I.   Relational Initiation
        A.   First Moves
        B.   Small Talk
        C.   Suggestion for Initiating Relationships

II.   From Initiation to Development
        A.   Self-Disclosure
                1.   Reciprocal
                2.   In Relationships
                3.   Self-Disclosure and Self-Knowledge
        B.   Social Penetration
                1.   Breadth
                2.   Depth
        C.   Influences on Self Disclosure
        D.   Suggestions for Self Disclosure in Relationships
        E.   Rhetorical Sensitivity
                1.   Noble Selves
                2.   Rhetorical Reflectors
                3.   Rhetorically Sensitive
                        a.   Interaction Consciousness

III. Relational Confirmation
    A. Disconfirming Responses
        1. Indifferent
        2. Impervious
        3. Disqualifying
    B. Confirming Responses
        1. Recognition
        2. Acknowledgement
        3. Endorsement

IV. Adapting to Your Style
    A. Context
    B. Goal
    C. Receptivity and Responsiveness

TEACHING OBJECTIVES

▸ To emphasize the importance of small talk as a conversational skill in initial encounters.

▸ To explain the role of self-disclosure in forming interpersonal relationships and the factors influencing its use.

▸ To discuss the Johari Window as a model for understanding levels of self-disclosure in various relationships.

▸ To describe the social penetration model and its usefulness.

▸ To explain the concept of rhetorical sensitivity and how it can be used to reduce uncertainty in relational formation.

▸ To analyze the ways we confirm or disconfirm others and the impact of these behaviors on our relationships.

TOPICS FOR STUDENT JOURNAL ENTRIES OR ESSAY ASSIGNMENTS:

1. Think of a relationship you have with someone you trust; for example, a close friend, a spouse, a parent or a sibling. Recall a time when you disclosed something personal about yourself to that person. Did it have any effect on the relationship? How did it affect the level of trust with this person? How has the relationship changed since that instance?

2.   Write a letter to someone important to you. Disclose something you have wanted to tell them but have not. Think about this process of self disclosure as you write the letter. How will you approach the subject? How will you disclose this information depending on the nature of the relationship? How will this process change the relationship?

3.   Review the Social Penetration Theory as explained in the chapter. Analyze two relationships—one which primarily has breadth and one which primarily has depth. How does the breadth or depth reveal the level of the relationship?

4.   Review Littlejohn's five attributes of a rhetorically sensitive person. Think of someone who you think exemplifies these characteristics. What are some examples of actions or behaviors which correspond with Littlejohn's attributes? Analyze this person according to Littlejohn's attributes. Why is this person rhetorically sensitive?

IN-CLASS ACTIVITIES FOR STUDENTS:

1.   Pair up with a partner. Then discuss your unwritten rules of self-disclosure. For example, do you feel comfortable disclosing personal relationship information? Are there some aspects of your life you never openly discuss? Where do you draw the line? Discuss and compare these unwritten rules.

2.   Following the "tips for maintaining small talk" as outlined in the chapter, break into small groups to engage in small talk. Be sure to follow the tips directly and do not allow yourself to move beyond any small talk. After this exercise, discuss the process of small talk. How does small talk enhance or disrupt the communication process? What function or purpose does small talk serve in the process of interpersonal communication?

3.   Researchers have found that women disclose more with people they like; men disclose more with people they trust.

As a class, discuss the differences in focus. What factors would account for such differences? Are women less trusting than men? Are men less "open" than women?

4.   According to the research, women tend to disclose more than men. Is this true? If this is a true assessment, do sociological factors play a key role here? Are women more biologically/ psychologically adaptive to be more disclosing than men? Discuss in small groups. After 15-20 minutes, share responses.

5.   Melody Beattie, in her book The Language of Letting Go, states: "We do not want others to see who we really are." In small groups, discuss whether this statement seems accurate. Why do many people want to avoid letting others get to really know them? What are the risks? What are the rewards of opening ourselves up to others?

6.   As a class or in small groups, discuss Harriet Goldhor Lerner's contention that it is "hard to feel intimate with someone we disagree with...we commonly confuse 'closeness' with 'sameness' and view intimacy as the merging of two separate "I's" into one worldview." Could this be why so many relationships never get beyond the "small talk" stage? Is this an issue of <u>trust</u> or one of <u>self-knowledge</u>?

7.   In small groups, discuss what T.V. programs (sitcoms, for example) emphasize in communication—"small talk," "self-disclosure," "rhetorical sensitivity?" What type of communication style is predominant in shows like "Melrose Place," "Roseanne," and "Northern Exposure?" What style predominates in talk shows such as "Oprah Winfrey" and "Maury Povich?" Does such patterning on television enhance or diminish our own ability to use meaningful communication skills?

TEST QUESTIONS

<u>Multiple Choice</u>

5.1   "Small talk" is an important interpersonal skill in that it:

    a.   allows time to get to know someone.
    b.   provides information about another person.
    c.   generally touches on light and positive topics.
    d.   can reduce uncertainty about another person.
 * e.   all of the above

5.2   How we communicate is affected by:

    a.   personality.
    b.   culture.
    c.   society.
    d.   genetics.
 * e.   two or more of the above

5.3   One of the most successful strategies for learning about another person is through:

    a.   small talk.
    b.   hidden cues.
 * c.   self-disclosure.
    d.   trick questions.
    e.   eye contact.

5.4   "Self-disclosure" theory suggests that:

      a.   we all need to share secrets.
* b.   attraction is related to positive disclosures but not to negative disclosure.
      c.   attraction is irrelevant to positive or negative disclosures.
      d.   self-disclosure occurs only at the intimate level of a relationship.
      e.   when rewarded, the need for disclosure decreases.

5.5   "Self-disclosure," to be appropriate, is:

      a.   not random but ongoing.
      b.   concerned for what is going on between people.
      c.   creating a chance for improving a relationship.
      d.   takes account of the effect it will have on the other person.
* e.   all of the above

5.6   The _____ concept attempts to illustrate the levels of self-disclosure we have in different relationships.

* a.   Johari window
      b.   social penetration
      c.   peak communication
      d.   reflector
      e.   none of the above

5.7   The originators of the Johari window concept were:

      a.   Sydney Jourard and J.H. Berg.
      b.   Sydney Jourard and Stephen Littlejohn.
* c.   Joseph Luft and Harry Ingram.
      d.   John Powell and Irving Altman.
      e.   Roderick Hart and Don Burks.

5.8   A key concept of the "social penetration" theory is that:

      a.   communication is rapid and broad at superficial levels of information.
      b.   communication gets increasingly slower and more limited in areas such as emotions and self-esteem.
      c.   disclosure is a gradual, developmental process.
      d.   personality plays a key role in communication.
* e.   all of the above

5.9   According to Altman and Taylor, personality is organized in two ways:

      a.   formal and informal categories.
  * b.   depth and breadth dimensions.
      c.   open and hidden agendas.
      d.   horizontal and vertical dimensions.
      e.   positive and negative perceptions.

5.10   _____ theorized that communication takes place on five levels.

      a.   Robert Johari
      b.   Dalmas Taylor
      c.   Kenneth Cissna
  * d.   John Powell
      e.   Stephen Littlejohn

5.11   One of the following is not one of the "five levels of communication":

      a.   cliché conversation
      b.   reporting facts about others
  * c.   meditating
      d.   emotional communication
      e.   peak level communication

5.12   Nearly complete disclosure and empathy occur at the _____ level of communication.

      a.   cliché
      b.   reporting of information
      c.   meditation
      d.   "gut" or emotional
  * e.   peak

5.13   The self-disclosure theory of communication grew out of humanistic psychology and much of the research was based on people who were seeking some form of:

  * a.   psychotherapy.
      b.   release.
      c.   knowledge of communication theory.
      d.   love.
      e.   enabling.

5.14 An alternative communication approach which requires an adaptive approach to others that balances one person's self-interests with the interests of others is termed:

    a.   self-disclosure.
    b.   reciprocal communication.
* c.   rhetorical sensitivity.
    d.   confirmation.
    e.   none of the above

5.15 One type of communicator, as defined by Hart and Burks, who doesn't adjust his communication strategies for others and who sticks to his personal ideas is the:

    a.   self-righteous pragmatist.
* b.   noble self.
    c.   rhetorical reflector.
    d.   rhetorically sensitive.
    e.   free spirit.

5.16 People seek to be rhetorically sensitive when they:

    a.   accept personal complexity.
    b.   avoid rigidity.
    c.   seek balance.
    d.   seek appropriateness of situation.
* e.   all of the above

5.17 One's feeling of recognition and acceptance as a unique and valuable person is termed:

    a.   recognition.
* b.   confirmation.
    c.   idealization.
    d.   self-disclosure.
    e.   noble self.

5.18 A relationship implies an _____ to feel a sense of personhood.

    a.   endorsement
    b.   openness
    c.   independence
* d.   interdependence
    e.   none of the above

5.19   According to Cissna and Sieburg, three major types of disconfirming responses include:

      a.   denial, debasement and reflective patterning.
      b.   anger, denial and withdrawal.
  * c.   indifferent, impervious and disqualifying.
      d.   indifferent, entrenchment and denial.
      e.   aversion, withdrawal and abandonment.

5.20   A "disconfirming" message:

      a.   blames.
      b.   criticizes.
      c.   uses sarcasm.
      d.   denies.
  * e.   two or more of the above

5.21   To be truly effective interpersonally, one must consider:

      a.   who one is.
      b.   what roles one plays.
      c.   what expectations are held out for in relationships.
      d.   the appropriate communication strategy.
  * e.   all of the above

5.22   Appropriate self-disclosure in relationships is:

      a.   random.
      b.   ongoing.
      c.   contingent.
      d.   thoughtful and discerning.
  * e.   two or more of the above

5.23   _____ advanced the theory of "social penetration."

  * a.   Irwin Altman and Dalmas Taylor
      b.   Harry Ingram and Joseph Luft
      c.   Harry Ingram and John Powell
      d.   Stephen Littlejohn and John Powell
      e.   Roderick Hart and Don Burks

5.24   According to John Powell, self-disclosure:

        a.   is a universal value.
        b.   represents an interpersonal communication panacea.
        c.   is always appropriate.
     * d.   is situational and developmental.
        e.   none of the above

5.25   In the book, The Transparent Self, psychologist _____ suggests that in ideal relationships people allow others to experience them fully and are open to experiencing others fully.

        a.   Sigmund Freud
     * b.   Sydney Jourard
        c.   Carl Rogers
        d.   John Powell
        e.   Martin Buber

True or False

5.1   To be effective interpersonally, people select the combination of communication skills that work best for them.

     * a.   true
        b.   false

5.2   There are strategies to become an ideal interpersonal communicator.

        a.   true
     * b.   false

5.3   For better or for worse, when someone meets someone else for the first time, both develop impressions of each other that influence the chances this relationship has for growing or not growing.

     * a.   true
        b.   false

5.4   Most, if not all, of the information people receive about others comes from verbal cues.

        a.   true
     * b.   false

5.5   Another term for small talk is "scripted" conversation.

    * a.   true
       b.   false

5.6   In conversations with new acquaintances, people generally talk about superficial information such as the weather.

    * a.   true
       b.   false

5.7   Although small talk is largely a waste of time, most people never move beyond this level of interpersonal skill.

       a.   true
    * b.   false

5.8   Self-disclosure is seldom reciprocal.

       a.   true
    * b.   false

5.9   Men tend to disclose more than women.

       a.   true
    * b.   false

5.10   Weak relationships are characterized by the need to self-disclose.

       a.   true
    * b.   false

5.11   As a rule, people respond to people who respond.

    * a.   true
       b.   false

5.12   Risk is a key element of self-disclosure.

    * a.   true
       b.   false

5.13   In communicating with others, we're not usually aware of our motivations.

      a.   true
* b.   false

5.14   Generally speaking, the more you are open to the feedback of others and the more comfortable you are in letting others know you, the larger your "window" of disclosure.

* a.   true
      b.   false

5.15   Many communication theorists reject the self-disclosure method as necessary to develop interpersonalness in relationships.

* a.   true
      b.   false

5.16   Hart, Carlson and Eadie believe the three general types of communicators are genetically-determined.

* a.   true
      b.   false

5.17   The "noble selves" concept can be used as a behavioral choice useful to gain knowledge of others and therefore further develop relationships.

      a.   true
* b.   false

5.18   Continued relationship development requires a sense of self-disclosure by the other.

      a.   true
* b.   false

5.19   "Disconfirmation" is to ignore someone's communication or presence.

* a.   true
      b.   false

5.20   "Recognition," as a confirming response, is expressed to the degree to which partners accept each other's feelings as "true, accurate and okay."

      a.   true
* b.   false

5.21 Cissna and Sieburg suggest that "endorsement," in a confirming response, occurs when we make "direct and relevant responses" to another's communication.

    a.   true
 * b.   false

5.22 It is important always to be aware of the context of communication and to be aware that relational development can be hurt from ignoring context.

 * a.   true
    b.   false

5.23 We can't <u>make</u> another person have an interpersonal relationship with us.

 * a.   true
    b.   false

5.24 Reception and responsiveness is communicated by the sending and receiving of confirming messages.

 * a.   true
    b.   false

5.25 Withholding judgements allows people to consider what they really want from relationships, to gain more accurate perceptions and to study the best route to successful communication.

 * a.   true
    b.   false

Short Essays

5.1 Explain the self-disclosure approach in communication.

5.2 Explain the Johari window concept.

5.3 Describe, from the social penetration perspective, the roles played by breadth and depth of information in developing relationships.

5.4 Describe how "rhetorical sensitivity" is an effective alternative to self-disclosure.

5.5 "In order to see, I have to be willing to be seen."—Anonymous. Explain how this statement applies to the self-disclosure concept.

5.6   "People respond to people who respond."—Anonymous.
        Explain how this statement applies to the "reciprocal" approach to self-disclosure.

5.7   Discuss the concept of "confirmation."

5.8   Discuss your understanding of the "interdependence" concept of a healthy
        relationship.

5.9   Discuss at length how the use of "self-disclosure" on your part either enhanced or,
        perhaps, destroyed a relationship that you greatly valued. What were the
        circumstances?

5.10   Why is inhibited self-disclosure the hallmark of a weak relationship?

CHAPTER 6

WHAT IS LANGUAGE?: NEGOTIATING REALITY

CHAPTER SYNOPSIS

Language has a powerful, magical, even mystical quality about it. Language is how we share
our internal world with others—how we negotiate our interpersonal realities in daily life.

Among the various theories of language, two strands are prominent in the field of
communication. One deals with the centrality of the **symbol** in communication, and the other
views **language as an activity** that requires the understanding of certain rules.

In studying language it is important to understand **semantics**—how language comes to
have meaning. The relationship between word, thought and referent can be direct or arbitrary.
We negotiate our meanings with others in our daily actions.

Language is also important in how we form our sense of who we are—our **self-identity**.
Basil Bernstein has identified certain "critical socializing contexts" in which our culture and
sense of self are passed on in seemingly insignificant conversations.

Our **perception** of the world we live in is largely related to our use and understanding
of language. Language is an activity we take part in from our time in our mother's womb
until the day we die. People simmer in a sort of "linguistic soup." To take part in the activity
of language we need to understand the pragmatics of language; that is, what we are using
language to accomplish. W. Barnett Pearce and Vernon Cronin have proposed their theory

"**coordinated management of meaning**" to suggest how each of us acquires clusters of rules that allow us to engage in language use. Our knowledge of rules develops our **communication competence**.

General semantics has provided some insights into dealing with language in our daily lives. Three key ideas are: language is not neutral; words are at various levels of abstraction; and people use language in habitual ways. Three skills help in our use of language in interpersonal contexts: (1) **sensitivity to others**, (2) **clarity of expression**, (3) **flexibility in meanings and attitude**, and (4) **appropriateness**.

CHAPTER OUTLINE

I.   What is Language?
   A.   Language is Symbolic
   B.   Language is Arbitrary
   C.   Words Have Different Kinds of Meaning
      1.   Connotative
      2.   Denotative
   D.   Words are at Various Levels of Abstraction
   E.   Language is Rule-Governed
   F.   Language Influences Reality
   G.   Language Influences Culture and Identity
      1.   Elaborated Codes
      2.   Restricted Codes
   H.   Words Actively Influence Roles and Relationship

II.   Language Negotiates Relational Reality
   A.   Coordinated Management of Meaning
      1.   Constitutive Rules
      2.   Regulative Rules
   B.   Negotiating Reality

III. Becoming a Critical Language Negotiator
   A.   Sensitivity
   B.   Clarity
   C.   Flexibility
   D.   Appropriateness

TEACHING OBJECTIVES

‣   To emphasize the importance of language to self-identity and interpersonal relationships.

- To present the notion of language and semiotic potential.

- To describe the relationship between language, perception and experience.

- To explain the concept of speech acts and the coordinated management of meaning in negotiating our realities with others.

- To emphasize the language skills of clarity of expression, sensitivity to others, and flexibility in attitudes and meanings.

TOPICS FOR STUDENT JOURNAL ENTRIES OR ESSAY ASSIGNMENTS:

1.	Describe a situation in which you were satisfied with the way you used language—perhaps in a conflict, problem or presentation. How did you use language to effectively communicate? Think of a situation in which you had difficulty using language. How could you have improved?

2.	List your personal strengths and weaknesses in your communication through language. For example, do your strengths lie with your vocabulary, choice of words, grammar, or perhaps your voice? Why do you think you are strong or weak in these areas?

3.	Compare and contrast how one person may use language differently depending on the situation. For example, a wife may speak differently to her husband than she does as the mother of a two-year-old. Think of how you use language in different situations. Compare and contrast your use of language.

4.	Re-read the section in the chapter on insensitive patterns of language. Describe a time when you may have been insensitive in your language. How could you have changed your own language behavior to be more sensitive?

IN-CLASS ACTIVITIES FOR STUDENTS:

1.	Think of a list of words which have changed in meaning in your lifetime. Discuss how these words have changed and the variety of meanings they have taken on over time. For example, the words "gay" and "cool" have taken on more than one meaning. See how many of these words your group can come up with. How do these changes reflect changes in society?

2.	As a group, think of two lists of terms which reflect neutral language vs. emotion-laden language. For example, "stingy" might be considered an emotion-laden term, but "thrifty" might come across as more neutral, or "snobby" vs. "independent." How do these lists reflect how language conveys values?

3.   Bring to class samples of "inaccurate translations" of language. An example would be: "You are invited to take advantage of the chambermaid."—posted at a Tokyo hotel front desk. Share these with the class. How is perception affected by language?

4.   Regarding self-identity, develop a symbol or logo to represent yourself. The logo should include a name and design. Provide some sample logos (e.g. Coca Cola, Planter's Peanuts, etc.) Share with the class your logo and an explanation for the choice of that particular logo.

5.   Discuss how sensitivity to others is a vital component of language. Is it a "responsibility?" Why or why not?

6.   Ask international students in the class to share how we unintentionally "butcher" their language. What do they find difficult about learning our language (e.g. dialects, accents, use of slang)?

7.   As a class or in two larger groups, discuss how concept of self varies from society to society and also from language to language (e.g. the self as a part of nature versus the self as separate from nature and a thing apart).

TEST QUESTIONS

<u>Multiple Choice</u>

6.1   The study of the use of signs and symbols as people construct, reconstruct, and even deconstruct the world is termed:

    a.   symbolism.
    b.   language.
* c.   semiotic potential.
    d.   semantics.
    e.   codefication.

6.2   It can be stated that through language:

    a.   links between humans are made through the use of signs and symbols.
    b.   problems can develop since language is a two-edged sword.
    c.   the internal world becomes externalized.
    d.   people share realities and negotiate meanings with others.
* e.   all of the above

6.3　　A _____ is something that stands for and refers arbitrarily to something else.

* a.　symbol
  b.　sign
  c.　behavior
  d.　code
  e.　none of the above

6.4　　A _____ points something out.

  a.　symbol
* b.　sign
  c.　behavior
  d.　code
  e.　none of the above

6.5　　_____ is the study of meanings.

  a.　Symbols
  b.　Sign language
  c.　Codes
* d.　Semantics
  e.　Linguistics

6.6　　According to Halliday, the interpersonal functions of language include:

  a.　the grammar of personal participation.
  b.　to adopt a role or a set of roles.
  c.　self-expression.
  d.　an active social process of discovery.
* e.　all of the above

6.7　　The person who theorized how language and social class are typified by codes was:

  a.　M.A.K. Halliday.
  b.　Socrates.
  c.　Kenneth Burke.
* d.　Basil Bernstein.
  e.　George Bernard Shaw.

6.8   A type of code which is generally longer, grammatically complex and flexible and associated with middle-class speech patterns in homes and schools:

    * a.   elaborated code
      b.   restricted code
      c.   language code
      d.   regulative code
      e.   none of the above

6.9   Language is:

      a.   symbol and meaning.
      b.   rule-governed.
      c.   an activity—a behavior.
      d.   a key element in the formation of self-identity.
    * e.   all of the above

6.10   "Speech acts" occur when:

      a.   language creates meaning.
    * b.   we intend language to do certain things for us.
      c.   we speak and gesture.
      d.   we pantomime as a form of communication.
      e.   none of the above

6.11   _____ and _____ have suggested that people learn through observation and practice.

      a.   Kenneth Burke and Edward Sapir
      b.   Bud Hazel and John Kelmer
    * c.   W. Barnett Pearce and Vernon Cronen
      d.   Basil Bernstein and S.I. Hayakawa
      e.   John Stewart and John Searle

6.12   The theory of the "coordinated management of meaning" (CMM) states that:

      a.   language is a series of symbols.
      b.   all languages share similar meaning.
      c.   language is abstract.
    * d.   we know how to use language because we follow rules that tell us how to understand and produce speech acts.
      e.   all of the above.

6.13   "Regulative rules":

    a.   signify signs and symbols.
    b.   tell us how to recognize speech acts.
* c.   identify in any given context the speech acts that are appropriate or not.
    d.   regulate our speech etiquette.
    e.   none of the above

6.14   The Sapir-Whorf hypothesis states that:

    a.   language is culture, and culture is controlled by and controls language.
    b.   language determines reality.
    c.   what we believe to be real is based on the language we habitually speak.
    d.   language is overly complicated.
* e.   two or more of the above

6.15   _____ is an area of communication that looks at how our behavior and attitudes are influenced by language and meanings.

* a.   General semantics
    b.   Codes elaborated
    c.   Symbols
    d.   Language potential
    e.   Communication competence

6.16   General semanticists study:

    a.   the history of languages.
    b.   symbol-referent relationships.
    c.   the behavior and results of language habits.
    d.   multiple meanings in language.
* e.   two or more of the above

6.17   _____, a general semanticist, formulated the "abstraction ladder."

    a.   Hadley Cantril
* b.   S.I. Hayakawa
    c.   John Condon
    d.   Vernon Cronen
    e.   none of the above

6.18   The _____ concept helps us to be aware of the level of language we are using and the degree of specificity we want.

        a.   semiotic potential
        b.   elaborated codes
    *   c.   abstraction ladder
        d.   Sapir-Whorf hypothesis
        e.   communication competence

6.19   A necessary skill in the use of language in interpersonal contexts is:

    *   a.   sensitivity to others.
        b.   a constant view of reality.
        c.   critical judgements.
        d.   separating the process world into discrete elements.
        e.   all of the above

6.20   By "talking the same language" of the receiver, it is meant that:

        a.   we mimic the language of the receiver.
    *   b.   we use/<u>choose</u> words appropriate for the listeners' level of abstraction.
        c.   we become highly multi-lingual.
        d.   we adapt the behavior of the receiver.
        e.   none of the above

6.21   The two instruments of communication which help people reach their "semiotic potential" are:

    *   a.   language and nonverbal behavior.
        b.   sign and symbol.
        c.   sensitivity and clarity of expression.
        d.   elaborated and restrictive codes.
        e.   constitutive and regulative rules.

6.22   A set of constitutive and regulative rules allows a person to:

        a.   understand language patterns.
    *   b.   interpret other people's acts and to translate these meanings into felt obligations to perform actions of one's own.
        c.   control his world.
        d.   construct reality.
        e.   none of the above

6.23   Through learning interpersonal functions of language, people:

      a.   adopt a set of roles.
      b.   accept or reject roles assigned to them.
      c.   express their own judgements and attitudes.
      d.   exert certain effects on receivers.
    * e.   all of the above

6.24   A person who speaks only one language is termed:

    * a.   monolingual.
      b.   bilingual.
      c.   trilingual.
      d.   multilingual.
      e.   nonlingual.

6.25   A common language trap is:

      a.   arbitrary language.
      b.   too many rules.
      c.   language is neutral.
    * d.   words are at various levels of abstraction.
      e.   none of the above

True or False

6.1   We use language to negotiate realty in our daily life.

    * a.   true
      b.   false

6.2   Understanding of human behavior is intricately linked with knowledge of language.

    * a.   true
      b.   false

6.3   Linguists and philosophers down through the centuries have identified language as the greatest accomplishment of humankind.

    * a.   true
      b.   false

6.4   Language, as we know it, began approximately 15,000,000 (15 million) years ago.

        a.   true
    * b.   false

6.5   Language is arbitrary.

    * a.   true
        b.   false

6.6   Meanings reside in objects and are codefied by receivers.

        a.   true
    * b.   false

6.7   The word is the thing.

        a.   true
    * b.   false

6.8   Language is rule governed.

    * a.   true
        b.   false

6.9   Generally, restrictive codes can be used to indicate who is a member of a group and who is not.

    * a.   true
        b.   false

6.10   Constrictive rules identify in any given context the speech acts that are appropriate or not.

        a.   true
    * b.   false

6.11   The ability to understand and use constitutive and regulative rules is called "communication competence."

    * a.   true
        b.   false

6.12   Conflicts and tension can occur if we misunderstand contexts or have inadequate sets of rules.

   * a.   true
     b.   false

6.13   People use language to describe what they perceive in their environment.

   * a.   true
     b.   false

6.14   Language influences self-concept but does not alter behavior and attitudes significantly.

     a.   true
   * b.   false

6.15   A bilingual person has a narrower view of the world than a monolingual person.

     a.   true
   * b.   false

6.16   "Reframing" is the process of changing the thinking by changing terms.

   * a.   true
     b.   false

6.17   According to John Condon, language reflects a point of view.

   * a.   true
     b.   false

6.18   Language is neutral.

     a.   true
   * b.   false

6.19   Language should be guided by the use of humor and trust.

   * a.   true
     b.   false

6.20   Stereotyping is unavoidable and it helps us to process and compartmentalize our sense of reality.

      a.   true
   * b.   false

6.21   To help achieve clarity of expression, whenever possible, "talk the same language" as your receiver.

   * a.   true
      b.   false

6.22   "Allness" language allows us to feel as one with other people.

      a.   true
   * b.   false

6.23   Flexibility in language usage and understanding is important; either-or attitudes are to be avoided.

   * a.   true
      b.   false

6.24   We tend to take language and the logic embedded within the structure of language for granted.

   * a.   true
      b.   false

6.25   What we ever "know" is limited by factors such as time, place, information and experience.

   * a.   true
      b.   false

Short Essays

6.1   Explain the importance of language in interpersonal relationships.

6.2   Describe the relationship between language and experience.

6.3   The quotation at the introduction to this chapter states: "Language is an expression of...what we give value to."—M.A.K. Halliday. What could this mean?

6.4   How are language and self-identity intertwined?

6.5   Explain Stewart's "potter's wheel" concept in negotiating realities.

CHAPTER 7

NONVERBAL BEHAVIOR AND COMMUNICATION RELATIONSHIPS

CHAPTER SYNOPSIS

Nonverbal behaviors are the signals, intentional, or unintentional, without the use of words, of any given sender. While some best-selling, popular books have tried to offer a short-cut to understanding human motivation and interaction, nonverbal communication is a complex subject.

Nonverbal modes of communication constitute, along with verbal skills, the **"communication package"** and are part of the **"semiotic potential."** This development continues over one's lifetime.

While it is difficult to separate verbal and nonverbal phenomena, nonverbal phenomena can be characterized in a variety of ways. Further, nonverbal communication serves a variety of **functions** in social interaction. These functions operate through the various communication channels of voice (**paralinguistics**), body movement (**kinesics**), physical space (**proxemics**), touching behavior (**haptics**), and more.

To be an effective communicator, one needs to become receptive to nonverbal cues in understanding someone's total series of messages. Three primary skills—**sensitivity**, **receptivity**, and **accurate comprehension**—which deal with receiving and sending nonverbal messages, are needed to control one's nonverbal messages and avoid sending unintentional or incongruent messages.

Because it is so important to avoid sending unintentional or incongruent messages, one needs to carefully attend to interactions. Knowing which nonverbal mode to use is every bit as important as carefully selecting the words. Nonverbal competence pays a high reward in avoiding misunderstandings, enhancing self-esteem, and gaining the esteem of others.

CHAPTER OUTLINE

I.   What is Nonverbal Behavior?
      A.   Nonverbal Behavior is Complex
      B.   Nonverbal Behavior is Important to Interpersonal Relationships

II.   The Communication Package: Your Semiotic Potential
      A.   Characteristics of Nonverbal Communication
            1.   Nonverbal Communication is On-Going
            2.   Nonverbal Communication can be Intentional or Unintentional
            3.   Nonverbal Communication is our Primary Mode for Expressing Emotions
            4.   Nonverbal Communication is Ambiguous
            5.   Nonverbal Communication Adumbrates Social Interaction
            6.   Nonverbal Communication is Culture Based
            7.   Nonverbal Messages are More Believable

      B.   The Functions of Nonverbal Communication in Social Interaction
            1.   Repeating
            2.   Substituting
            3.   Adding Detail or Complementing
            4.   Accenting
            5.   Contradicting

III. The Nonverbal Repertoire
      A.   Paralinguistics
      B.   Kinesics and Eye Behavior
            1.   Emblems
            2.   Illustrators
            3.   Regulators
            4.   Affect Displays
            5.   Adaptors
      C.   Eye Behavior or Gaze
            1.   Mutual Gaze
            2.   Avoidance
            3.   Gaze Aversion
            4.   Predatory Gaze
      D.   Proxemics
            1.   Interpersonal Zones
            2.   Breaking The Rules
            3.   Territoriality
      E.   Haptics or Touching Behavior
      F.   Physical Characteristics
      G.   Artifactual Communication
      H.   Chronemics or Temporal Communication

IV.   Sensitivity, Receptivity, and Accurate Comprehension
        A.   Conscious Feedback
        B.   Attitude

V.   Sending Nonverbal Messages With Clarity

TEACHING OBJECTIVES

▶   To explore the connection between verbal and nonverbal communication in reaching
        our semiotic potential.

▶   To contrast nonverbal behavior and nonverbal communication.

▶   To provide a definition of nonverbal behavior and its role in interpersonal
        relationships.

▶   To present examples of congruent and incongruent nonverbal communication.

▶   To discuss methods for more accurately conveying nonverbal messages and for more
        accurately understanding nonverbal messages received.

TOPICS FOR STUDENT JOURNAL ENTRIES OR ESSAY ASSIGNMENTS:

1.   Observe a conversation, paying attention to only the non-verbal aspects of the
communication. Discuss all the non-verbal communication. What does it reveal about the
relationship and topic of conversation?

2.   Respond to the discussion on somatypes in the chapter. Do you agree with the
conclusions about character qualities based on body types? Can you think of an example
where this is true? Can you think of exceptions to this "rule?"

3.   Think of a relationship in your life. What are some non-verbal communication
activities which are specific to that relationship? For example, are there knowing glances, a
particular touch or a facial expression which is exclusively a reflection of that relationship?

4.   Think of a time where there was a conflict between someone's (or yours) actions and
words. Describe the situation. Which spoke louder—the actions or the words? How was this
discrepancy revealed? Was it ever resolved? If so, how?

IN-CLASS ACTIVITIES FOR STUDENTS:

1.   In pairs, get up and move closer to each other while engaging in a conversation. Ask the other to stop when they feel they are at a comfortable distance. Tell them to move even closer. Ask them how they feel now. Discuss how use of personal space could reflect one's culture or define a relationship.

2.   Think back on your family life as you were growing up. How important was touch to your family? Discuss how your family values and uses (or doesn't use) touch. Have you been affected/influenced by your family's conditioning? In what way?

3.   In small groups, discuss how two different cultures/societies use proxemics differently than in our U.S. society. After 15 minutes of discussion, compare observations with the class.

4.   Pair off with a class member. Tell each other some general biographical information about yourself. After 2 minutes for each participant to relay information, write a brief "personality perception profile" based on your perception of your partner's voice qualities and other nonverbal behavior cues. Allow 10 minues for writing. Return to original pairings and share impressions with each other. Keep it light! Do the perceptions seem similar or very different?

5.   As an exercise in gender perception, do reverse role-play for the following hypothetical situations:
   a.   Two female friends meeting for lunch to share confidences.
   b.   Two male friends meeting for lunch to share confidences.
   c.   Four women sitting around a card table, playing cards.
   d.   Four men sitting around a card table, playing cards.
   e.   A woman greeting her sister at the airport after a year's absence.
   f.   A man greeting his sister at the airport after a year's absence.

As a class, discuss the nonverbal cues used in each scenario. Did these nonverbal cues differ significantly in how the men and women actually react in these given situations, or in how they <u>perceive</u> that they react in such given situations? What are the sources of these perceptions? What are women's perceptions of men's "typical" nonverbal behavior? What are men's perceptions of women's "typical" nonverbal behavior?

6.   What are some U.S. professions that have standard emblems associated with them? (For example, ground controllers use gestures to direct pilots into proper position.) What emblems do we identify with another culture? Are some emblems universal?

7.   As a class, discuss how interactions are affected by the intensity of a person's voice during an interaction. Give examples of positive or negative reactions to various voice intensities and their relevance. For example, with the command, "I want you to come here!" How would this or that voice intensity affect the perception (and likely outcome) of the receiver toward the speaker?

8.   As a class or in smaller groupings, discuss whether men and women in our culture (U.S.) tend to demonstrate different touching behaviors (haptics). If so, do these behaviors seem to be essentially cultural or biologically determined?

TEST QUESTIONS

<u>Multiple Choice</u>

7.1   What term below best describes the following: "Those attributes or actions of humans, other than the use of words themselves, which have socially shared meaning, and have potential for feedback from the receiver."

      a.   posturing
* b.   nonverbal behavior
      c.   sign language
      d.   communication interaction
      e.   neutral expressionism

7.2   _____ occurs when signals, intentional or unintentional, are perceived and assigned meaning.

      a.   Nonverbal behavior
* b.   Nonverbal communication
      c.   Verbal linkage
      d.   Interpretation
      e.   none of the above

7.3   Some components of the communication package include:

* a.   visual, tactile and olfactory.
      b.   psychology, sociology and anthropology.
      c.   the arts, the sciences, languages.
      d.   linguistics, semantics, communications.
      e.   none of the above

7.4   Which of the following is <u>not</u> a form of nonverbal message?

      a.   facial expressions
      b.   body movements
      c.   vocal qualities/tone
* d.   singing
      e.   distances between interactants

7.5   Nonverbal communication is:

        a.   ongoing.
        b.   intentional or unintentional.
        c.   the primary mode for expressing emotions.
        d.   ambiguous.
    * e.   all of the above

7.6   The book, <u>The Expression of Emotions in Man and Animals</u>, was the beginning of the scientific era of study of nonverbal communication. Who was the author of this book?

        a.   Judee Burgoon
        b.   Julius Fast
    * c.   Charles Darwin
        d.   M.A.K. Halliday
        e.   Ray Birdwhistell

7.7   Adumbrative cues operate:

        a.   outside awareness.
        b.   at both the interpersonal and small-group levels of communication.
        c.   to tell us when to proceed.
        d.   to tell us how to proceed.
    * e.   two or more of the above

7.8   According to Ekman, the primary functions of nonverbal messages are:

    * a.   repeating, substituting, complementing, accenting and contradicting.
        b.   expressing, receiving, manipulating, advising.
        c.   understanding and function.
        d.   action and reaction.
        e.   expression and reaction.

7.9   In nonverbal communication, sounds accompanying speech such as laughing and crying are termed:

        a.   behavior cues.
    * b.   paralinguistics.
        c.   verbalization.
        d.   communication utterances.
        e.   exclamations.

7.10   In a major study by D.W. Addington, males with a nasal quality to their voice are generally perceived as:

    * a.   socially undesirable overall.
      b.   masculine and dynamic.
      c.   more animated and extroverted.
      d.   older, cantankerous and unyielding.
      e.   younger and more effeminate.

7.11   In the same study by Addington, females with a throaty quality to their voices are perceived as:

      a.   more feminine and high strung.
      b.   immature and more withdrawn.
    * c.   less intelligent, more masculine and lazier.
      d.   younger and more emotional.
      e.   none of the above

7.12   To _____ is to foreshadow or to partially disclose.

      a.   verbalize
    * b.   adumbrate
      c.   whisper
      d.   explain
      e.   none of the above

7.13   A term for body movements such as gestures, posture and movement including eye behavior is:

      a.   personality cues.
      b.   paralanguage.
      c.   adaptive behavior.
    * d.   kinesics.
      e.   communication tools.

7.14   According to Ekman and Friesen, there are basically five types of body expressions. Which of the following is not one of those five types of expression?

      a.   emblems
      b.   illustrators
      c.   regulators
    * d.   deregulators
      e.   affect displays

7.15   A(n) _____ is the gestural equivalent of a word or phrase.

        a.   hallmark
        b.   social expression
        c.   adaptor
        d.   illustrator
   * e.   emblem

7.16   Movements in which people point to an object to which they are verbally referring to are _____.

        a.   emblems
   * b.   illustrators
        c.   affect displays
        d.   adaptors
        e.   none of the above

7.17   Adaptors are movements, learned in _____, that are part of a patterned activity.

   * a.   childhood
        b.   adolescence
        c.   adulthood
        d.   social situations
        e.   cultural grooming

7.18   The study of _____ has to do with personal and physical space in nonverbal behavior.

        a.   kinesics
        b.   aesthetics
        c.   regulators
   * d.   proxemics
        e.   haptics

7.19   According to Edward Hall, which of the following variable affects social interaction in interpersonal communication?

        a.   gender and posture
        b.   use of touch
        c.   visual contact
        d.   voice loudness
   * e.   all of the above

7.20   _____ include all those artifacts or elements you add to your body such as jewelry, hairpieces and perfumes.

      a.   Affect displays
      b.   Adumbrates
      c.   Emblems
      d.   Haptics
* e.   none of the above

7.21   A key to accurate comprehension and understanding nonverbal messages is:

      a.   artifactual communication.
* b.   conscious feedback.
      c.   the use of affect display.
      d.   the use of illustrators.
      e.   the use of adaptors.

7.22   Kelly-Dyreson, Burgan and Bailey found in studying nonverbal messages that:

* a.   females are superior to males in nonverbal sensitivity.
      b.   females have greater intelligence than males.
      c.   accuracy is greater in the localic channel than in decoding kinesic channels.
      d.   females handle stress better than males.
      e.   two or more of the above

7.23   As a sender of nonverbal messages, controlling one's nonverbal messages is possible:

      a.   100% of the time.
* b.   most of the time.
      c.   seldom.
      d.   never.
      e.   any of the above, depending on circumstances.

7.24   How sensitive and receptive people are in interpreting nonverbal signals is influenced by:

      a.   haptics.
      b.   artifactual communication.
      c.   feedback.
* d.   attitude.
      e.   proxemics.

7.25   Sending nonverbal messages with clarity requires:

        a.   conscious effort.
        b.   sensitivity to others.
        c.   receptivity.
        d.   accurate comprehension.
   * e.   all of the above

True or False

7.1   People can engage in nonverbal communication only in the presence of someone else who chooses to interpret their behavior as messages and assign meanings to them.

   * a.   true
     b.   false

7.2   Trying to separate nonverbal and verbal messages ignores the true relationship and understanding of verbal and nonverbal behavior.

   * a.   true
     b.   false

7.3   Generally, we can recognize whether people are intentionally or unintentionally sending a message.

     a.   true
   * b.   false

7.4   The study of nonverbal behavior has been popularized in the last twenty years.

   * a.   true
     b.   false

7.5   Psychologist Albert Mehrabian has suggested that more than 85 percent of every message is translated through nonverbal channels.

     a.   true
   * b.   false

7.6   The "communication package" develops over a lifetime.

   * a.   true
     b.   false

7.7   We can choose to stop talking, but we can't stop communicating.

   * a.   true
     b.   false

7.8   Because nonverbal signals are visible, they're beyond ready concealment or manipulation.

   * a.   true
     b.   false

7.9   Communication takes place only in the reception and interpretation of the message.

   * a.   true
     b.   false

7.10   Early studies of facial expression were for the study of emotional expression and survival values.

     a.   true
   * b.   false

7.11   The tone and inflection of your voice in itself carries a message.

   * a.   true
     b.   false

7.12   Body gestures are repressed nonverbal communicators.

     a.   true
   * b.   false

7.13   Emblematic movements most frequently occur when the verbal channel is blocked.

   * a.   true
     b.   false

7.14   Emblems, like language, are learned in everyday social interaction and for the most part are culturally nonspecific.

     a.   true
   * b.   false

7.15   Illustrators are for the most part intentional acts.

    * a.   true
       b.   false

7.16   Illustrators can only be understood in connection with the verbal message.

       a.   true
    * b.   false

7.17   Regulators are body expressions that reflect the emotional state of the communicator.

       a.   true
    * b.   false

7.18   Affect displays tend to be less consciously controllable than other types of body expression.

    * a.   true
       b.   false

7.19   When people are talking together, their use of adaptors can be a distraction from really engaging in communication.

    * a.   true
       b.   false

7.20   "Gaze avoidance" is the practice, common among people in normal conversation, of looking at the speaker or receiver at times and at other times looking away.

       a.   true
    * b.   false

7.21   Even in mainstream U.S. culture, a direct stare is considered a social offense to be avoided.

    * a.   true
       b.   false

7.22   The cultural anthropologist Edward T. Hall found that the amount of space people leave between themselves and others is to a great extent culturally determined.

    * a.   true
       b.   false

7.23   "Haptics" is concerned with the tendency to use fixed geographical space as one's own territory or untouchable space.

     a.   true
* b.   false

7.24   In interpersonal relationships, the size and location of territory indicates status.

* a.   true
     b.   false

7.25   The degree to which someone is satisfied with a relationship has little real influence on how they interpret another's nonverbal communication.

     a.   true
* b.   false

7.26   Studies by Robert Rosenthal showed that females are better at detecting nonverbal cues.

* a.   true
     b.   false

Short Essays

7.1   "Actions speak louder than words." What does this expression mean to you based on your experience with someone in the past few weeks?

7.2   How are proxemics a result of a cultural norm?

7.3   List 8 body movements with a generally negative connotation in our society (Anglo-American). List 8 body movements with a generally positive connotation in our society.

7.4   How can nonverbal communication be ambiguous? Be specific.

7.5   Explain in a paragraph what can happen when people miss nonverbal cues.

7.6   How does eye behavior affect communication perception?

7.7   What distracting mannerisms do you have? Do others make you aware of these mannerisms? What mannerisms would you like to eradicate? Why?

7.8   List 10 "emblems" not cited in the text in our U.S. culture. What do they signify? List 10 "emblems" in one or more other cultures which are foreign to our culture. Identify the culture to which each of the last 10 "emblems" belong and what they signify.

7.9   How do you "typically" display negative emotion? List 5-10 "affect displays" that you know you commonly employ. Specifically, which nonverbal cues are used to communicate the following emotions:

- anger
- disappointment
- fear
- sadness, depression
- disgust

7.10   What is your comfort level with touching behavior? Are you <u>basically</u> a "touchy, feely" person or a "don't touch, don't get too close" type of person? Have you always been so?

CHAPTER 8

LISTENING

CHAPTER SYNOPSIS

Effective listening goes hand in hand with effective interpersonal communication. Poor listeners are usually poor communicators. At least four kinds of listening can help students improve their skills: informational, empathic, critical and dialogic.

Active informational listeners try to understand what someone else is saying. **Passive** listeners, on the other hand, often tune out messages or hear only part of them. Ralph Nichols, among others, has listed some causes of poor listening. These include pretending to listen, listening only if a subject or speaker is interesting, and wasting the differential between thought speed and voice speed. Effective listeners focus on the message without regard to how interesting it might be. They use the thought speed, voice speed differential to their advantage. They also practice proven memory techniques to retain what they've heard.

An **empathic** listener tries to get into the perceptual world of someone else. Just as there are positive and negative ways to listen for information, the same is true for empathic listening. Poor empathic listeners tend to see situations only from their own perspective.

They fail to offer any kind of support to the other person. While empathic listening is a positive style, it can be overdone if one person totally loses herself in the other's feelings or point of view. Skilled empathic listeners keep a certain amount of objectivity as they attempt to understand and paraphrase the other's viewpoint.

This objectivity leads to a third kind of important listening, namely critical listening. Poor critical listeners are often more impressed with the status of the person conveying a message than they are with whether the message makes sense. They make incorrect inferences, are vulnerable to doublespeak and fail to seek out evidence of claims others make. Good critical listeners check to insure that claims are supported by evidence and logical inferences. They insist that statements be cogent.

A final kind of listening is **dialogic**. In this form of communication, both parties build ideas together as they listen to each other carefully. One makes a statement and the other draws on it. John Stewart refers to dialogic listening as "sculpting mutual meanings." Dialogic listening is characterized by open-endedness, concentration on the mutual "text" the two are shaping and a sense of playfulness.

CHAPTER OUTLINE

I.   Listening and Interpersonal Communication
      A.   How Listening is Different From Hearing

II.   Informational Listening
      A.   Poor Informational Listening Behaviors
            1.   Pseudo-listening
            2.   Tuning Out Because the Speaker or Topic is Boring
            3.   Wasting the Differential Between Thought-Speed and Voice-Speed
      B.   Better Ways to Listen For Information
            1.   Focus on Key Points Instead of Remembering Facts
            2.   Use the Thought-Speed/Voice-Speed Differential to Your Advantage
            3.   Use Effective Memory Methods to Absorb and Remember Information

III.   Empathic Listening
      A.   Types of Poor Empathic Listening
            1.   Unwillingness to See the Other Person's Side
            2.   Not Listening With Support
            3.   Being Too Empathic in Some Situations
      B.   Better Ways to Listen Empathically
            1.   Paraphrasing
            2.   Keeping Some Sense of Objectivity

IV. Critical Listening
    A. Faults of Critical Listening
        1. Focusing on Status Rather than Ideas
        2. Falling for Doublespeak
        3. Being Overly Critical
        4. Incorrect Inferences
        5. Failure to Look For Evidence to Support Claims
    B. Better Ways to Listen Critically
        1. Check to See if Claims Are Supported With Evidence
        2. Make Sure That the Reasoning You Hear is Cogent
        3. Insist on Correct Inferences

V. Dialogic Listening
    A. "Ours" Instead of "Mine"
        1. Open-ended and Playful
        2. In Front Rather than Behind
        3. Presentness

TEACHING OBJECTIVES

▸ To emphasize the importance of listening in interpersonal relationships and why listening is often difficult.

▸ To clarify the difference between listening and hearing.

▸ To explore the four kinds of listening important for interpersonal effectiveness.

▸ To present ways listening skills can be improved.

TOPICS FOR STUDENT JOURNAL ENTRIES OR ESSAY ASSIGNMENTS:

1.   Think about your own listening skills. Are there any situations in which you have difficulty listening? What are some causes of poor listening for you? Do you have any particular patterns of listening? Think of some situations which illustrate your listening skills.

2.   Think of a situation where you had to engage in informational listening. Using the suggestions and ideas in the chapter, analyze your informational listening. What are your strengths and weaknesses in this area?

3.   Think of one person who you listen to often. Are you a critical listener? Do you commit any of the faults of critical listening covered in the chapter? How could you improve your critical listening skills with this person?

4.   Think of two people, one you would consider an empathic listener and one who you would not consider an empathic listener. Compare and contrast their listening behaviors. What does the empathic listener do that the other doesn't?

IN-CLASS ACTIVITIES FOR STUDENTS:

1.   Split into two groups. Select a controversial, debatable issue. One group should take one side of an issue and the other group take the opposite side. The two groups are to think of 3 to 4 arguments and conduct a debate format. The primary rule is that one team must paraphrase the other team's argument adequately before they can present their own argument. A neutral judge will facilitate this process to assure that both teams are satisfied with this listening and paraphrasing process.

2.   Prepare a short lecture on a topic relevant to the class. Prior to delivering the lecture, split the class into three groups. Ask one group to listen for facts and details, one group to listen for general ideas, and the last group to simply listen for enjoyment. After the lecture, ask each group to provide feedback. What did they retain from the lecture? What did they get out of it? What was their impression of the information? How did listening for different purposes change the information retained by each group?

3.   As an exercise in paraphrasing, cut out three brief articles from the newspaper and paraphrase each article in no more than 3-4 sentences. (Attach and turn in.)

4.   Split up into pairs. Provide autobiographic information to the other for three minutes each.

5.   Bring examples of "doublespeak" from magazine or newspaper articles, obituary notices, pamphlets or other sources to share with the class.

6.   Listen to a short segment of a well-known speech (i.e. Martin Luther King's "I have a Dream" speech) and write a paragraph summary of <u>what you hear</u> as key points contained in that part of the speech. In one sentence, what was his thesis statement?

7.   List (on paper) at least three kinds each of "active" and "passive" listening. For example, when we listen to music on the stereo, it is usually for relaxation and so is "passive." When we listen to the news on the radio or the T.V. set, it is generally to obtain information and so is "active" listening.

TEST QUESTIONS

<u>Multiple Choice</u>

8.1   Hearing words and understanding only a few ideas can be described as what kind of listening?

        a.   informational
        b.   empathic
        c.   active
    *   d.   passive
        e.   more than two of the above

8.2   Another term for "faking attention" is:

    *   a.   pseudo-listening.
        b.   artificial listening.
        c.   empathic listening.
        d.   critical listening.
        e.   none of the above

8.3   A listener who is preparing what he wants to say rather than absorbing the ideas of a partner is:

        a.   giving in to distractions.
        b.   failing to listen empathically.
    *   c.   wasting the differential between thought speed and voice speed.
        d.   focusing on the idea rather than the person.
        e.   tuning out.

8.4   Two components of memory are association and imagination. A last key element is:

        a.   empathy.
    *   b.   repetition.
        c.   critical listening.
        d.   pseudo listening.
        e.   regurgitation.
        f.   more than one of the above

8.5   A concise response to the speaker which states the essence of the others' content in a listener's own words can be described as:

      a.   listening objectively.
   * b.   paraphrasing.
      c.   listening with acute empathy.
      d.   relational listening.
      e.   critical listening.

8.6   Which of the following is not one of the four kinds of listening used in interpersonal communication?

   * a.   analytical
      b.   informational
      c.   empathic
      d.   critical
      e.   dialogic

8.7   Listening to acquire data is described as:

      a.   reflective listening.
      b.   passive listening.
   * c.   informational listening.
      d.   active listening.
      e.   critical listening.

8.8   In a study on listening in lectures by Professor Paul Cameron, it was found that, on the average, students paid attention:

      a.   8% of the time.
   * b.   20% of the time.
      c.   25% of the time.
      d.   45% of the time.
      e.   60% of the time.

8.9   The three methods of "remembering" are:

      a.   hearing, listening and analyzing.
      b.   hearing, listening and paraphrasing.
      c.   hearing, listening and retention.
   * d.   association, imagination and repetition.
      e.   association, repetition and paraphrasing.

8.10   Linking things such as ideas, places, and the like is referred to as:

      a.   references.
  * b.   association.
      c.   inferences.
      d.   paraphrasing.
      e.   none of the above

8.11   When we listen carefully to consider whether the ideas that are being discussed make sense or seem logical we are practicing:

  * a.   critical listening.
      b.   relational listening.
      c.   informal listening.
      d.   subjective listening.
      e.   informational listening.

8.12   An obstacle to careful listening is:

      a.   focusing on status rather than ideas.
      b.   being overly critical.
      c.   making incorrect inferences.
      d.   failing to look for supporting evidence.
  * e.   all of the above

8.13   An attempt to hide the truth with acceptable language is known as:

      a.   pseudo-talk.
      b.   paraphrasing.
  * c.   doublespeak.
      d.   inferences.
      e.   none of the above

8.14   "Sculpting mutual meanings" is a definition of:

      a.   critical listening.
      b.   relational listening.
  * c.   dialogic listening.
      d.   pseudo-listening.
      e.   empathic listening.

8.15   Which of the following is not a feature of dialogic listening?

      a.   seeing a situation from an "ours" perspective
* b.   being critical and narrowly-focused
      c.   avoiding focusing on "what is behind"
      d.   "presentness"
      e.   being open-minded and playful

8.16   "To attend closely" is to:

      a.   hear.
      b.   respond.
      c.   dialogue.
* d.   listen.
      e.   none of the above

8.17   One fault of empathic listening is:

* a.   getting overly involved.
      b.   becoming too critical.
      c.   receiving too much information at one time.
      d.   becoming bored.
      e.   the need to negate our own feelings.

8.18   A prominent author who coined the term "doublespeak" was:

      a.   William Bennett.
      b.   John Grisham.
* c.   George Orwell.
      d.   John Stewart.
      e.   John Milton.

8.19   In a "mutual sculpting of meaning" two partners:

      a.   create a new language system.
* b.   focus on the verbal and nonverbal text that the two are creating.
      c.   concentrate on the hidden meaning of words.
      d.   create an artistic work built on their mutual efforts.
      e.   marry.

8.20   We make an "incorrect inference" when we:

    a.   don't compile a whole series of data that leads to a probable conclusion.
    b.   jump to a hasty conclusion.
    c.   look at an inference and then draw a conclusion about what caused that experience.
    d.   don't consider mitigating circumstances.
*   e.   two or more of the above

True or False

8.1   Hearing and listening are the same.

    a.   true
*   b.   false

8.2   Faking attention and pseudo-listening are the same.

*   a.   true
    b.   false

8.3   Listeners are well advised to focus on key points instead of trying to remember isolated facts.

*   a.   true
    b.   false

8.4   Unwillingness to see the other person's side can be described as critical listening.

    a.   true
*   b.   false

8.5   You can never be too empathetic in listening to another person.

    a.   true
*   b.   false

8.6   Students listen with a 45% level of listening effectiveness.

    a.   true
*   b.   false

8.7   Studies have confirmed that we talk more than we listen during most encounters.

      a.   true
 * b.   false

8.8   You can think three to four times faster than you can talk.

 * a.   true
      b.   false

8.9   On the average, you speak between 100 and 150 words per minute.

 * a.   true
      b.   false

8.10   You can think at around 400 words per minute.

 * a.   true
      b.   false

8.11   The differential between thought-speed and voice-speed can be a liability or an asset.

 * a.   true
      b.   false

8.12   We need to listen to everything we hear.

      a.   true
 * b.   false

8.13   Words low on the abstraction ladder are easy to remember because they're vivid.

 * a.   true
      b.   false

8.14   Association and vivid imaging are methods too difficult to master.

      a.   true
 * b.   false

8.15   When it comes to empathic listening, our efforts will always be grounded in our own attitudes, expectations, past experiences and world view.

 * a.   true
      b.   false

8.16 We say reasoning is cogent when statements are logically convincing and are backed by some evidence.

   * a.   true
     b.   false

8.17 Dialogic listening requires that two people stay on a single topic.

     a.   true
   * b.   false

8.18 Dialogic listening can only involve two people at a given time.

     a.   true
   * b.   false

8.19 An "inference" is a logical leap from evidence to a conclusion.

   * a.   true
     b.   false

8.20 In "presentness," partners focus on the past so that they can build for the present on a solid base of understanding.

     a.   true
   * b.   false

Short Essays

8.1 You have rented an apartment near the campus for one year. Before moving in, the landlord demanded that you put down $300 as a deposit. You've kept the apartment meticulously clean and, in your opinion, you did no damage to any of the rooms. Your landlord says that he cannot refund the $300 damage deposit because of some peeled paint in the bathroom and some scuff marks on the floor. In your negotiation with him to get the money back, please demonstrate how all four kinds of listening—informational, empathic, critical and dialogic—might help you gain back your damage deposit.

8.2 How is dialogic listening different from critical and empathic listening? How is it the same?

8.3 List three ineffective ways that people listen. Using a personal experience, give an example for each type of ineffective listening. Why were these experiences ineffective?

8.4   When was the last time you engaged in"doublespeak?" What was the circumstance? Why did you feel it was necessary to use "doublespeak?"

8.5   Scott Peck states that "True listening is always a manifestation of love." How is this so?

8.6   Cite a personal example in which you were <u>too</u> empathic to someone and it proved to be a hinderance. What should have been the response?

8.7   How is pseudo-listening different from passive listening?

8.8   What are two effective memory methods which you use to absorb and remember information? Do you have a "unique" method for retaining what you want to remember? How does it work?

8.9   In dialogic listening, explain the concept of "in front of rather than behind." Why is the "in front of" more focusing than the "behind" approach?

8.10   In dialogic listening, what is meant by the "'ours' instead 'mine'" concept?

CHAPTER 9

CLOSE RELATIONSHIPS

CHAPTER SYNOPSIS

Close relationships with others can bring deep joy or cause intense pain. As such, they have profound impact on people's lives. An intimate union can be described as one in which participants share their innermost thoughts and feelings.

A number of scholars have explained why relationships develop and continue. Steve Duck notes that humans filter data over time to see if others might match them in attitudes or personality. William Shutz maintains that we get into close unions because of three needs: **inclusion, control** and **affection**. Thibault and Kelley propose a **social exchange** or **reward theory** to help explain attraction between two people who are moving closer to each other.

Mark Knapp has described discernible stages two people go through as they forge their relationship. These are initiation, experimentation, intensification, integration and bonding. Such steps are not static because a couple may go back and forth between the stages or they might experience "turning points." Leslie Baxter describes such turning points as "dialectic tensions" which include a need for both autonomy and connection, openness and closedness, as well as novelty and predictability.

One reason close unions are challenging is because women and men are brought up differently. Deborah Tannen has documented these differences and helps explain why they occur.

Couples who seem happiest after some years appear to emphasize five elements in an order of priority. The five are: shared values, friendship, compatible temperaments, romance and sexual attraction. The North American culture often encourages romance and sex as the major ingredients of a successful union and such an emphasis can create problems in long-term satisfaction.

All close relationships experience conflict, a phenomenon Hocker and Wilmot describe as an expressed struggle between two interdependent people who see incompatible goals, small rewards and interference from the other in achieving their goals. Reactions to conflict can range from destructive to positive.

Conflict poorly handled can lead to relationship disintegration. Knapp describes five stages of breakdown: differentiation, circumscribing, stagnation, avoidance, and termination.

Another type of close relationship is friendship—the union of two people who know each other well and who share strong affection. Unlike family situations where members are often given little choice, friends can choose each other. Argyle and Henderson suggest six characteristics that distinguish close from superficial friendships.

As in other types of unions, conflicts can occur between friends. Because good friends share psychological intimacy, they can usually work out problems easier than they can with colleagues or strangers. Friendships sometimes last and sometimes end for various reasons. Whether they continue or end, most friendships have made people's lives richer and thus are worth the investment they demand.

CHAPTER OUTLINE

I.   Intimate Relationships
       A.   Why Do Close Relationships Develop?
              1.   Needs
              2.   Rewards and Relationships
       B.   Stages in a Close Relationship
              1.   Initiating
              2.   Experimenting
              3.   Intensifying
              4.   Bonding
       C.   Tensions and Turning Points in a Relationship

D. Women and Men are Socially Conditioned in Different Ways: Why Can't a Man Be Like a Woman?
E. Elements of Successful Unions
    1. Shared Values
    2. Friendship
    3. Temperamental Compatibility
    4. Romantic Attraction or "Limerance"
    5. Sexual Attraction
F. Conflict in Close Relationships
    1. Destructive Approaches
    2. Advantages of Conflict
    3. Effective Ways to Handle Conflict
G. Mutual Problem Solving and Negotiation
H. Five Stages of Relationship Disintegration
    1. Differentiating
    2. Circumscribing
    3. Stagnating
    4. Avoiding
    5. Terminating

II. Friendship
  A. Foundations of Friendship
  B. Conflict Between Friends
  C. Why Do Some Friendships End?

TEACHING OBJECTIVES

▸ To clarify the similarities and differences between intimate relationships and friendships.

▸ To explain how close relationships develop.

▸ To explore the role of conflict in close relationships and differentiate between constructive and destructive confrontations.

▸ To describe the stages of relationship initiation, maintenance, and termination.

▸ To present communication strategies that will enhance rather than hinder close unions.

TOPICS FOR STUDENT JOURNAL ENTRIES OR ESSAY ASSIGNMENTS:

1.   Think about a friendship you had in the past which is now over. Why did this friendship end? How do you feel about this person now? Do you regret this friendship's termination?

2.   Think about a close relationship in your life. After reviewing the stages of a close relationship, discuss how this relationship may or may not have progressed through some or all of these stages. Which stages have you gone through? What stage are you in now? Where do you see this relationship going?

3.   Think of one relationship which has ended. Write about this disintegration process using the five stages of relationship disintegration in the chapter. What are your overall feelings about this disintegration? How do your feelings relate to the stages? For example, do you generally feel bad or good because of a completed stage? Or did the disintegration skip some stages which affect your feelings?

4.   Review the elements of a successful union as outlined in the chapter. Think of someone with whom you believe you have a successful union. Are these elements present in your relationship? Discuss this relationship according to those elements.

IN-CLASS ACTIVITIES FOR STUDENTS:

1.   In small groups, discuss how you handle conflict in close relationships. Think of specific examples of conflict behaviors. What do you do well? What do you do poorly? How could you improve these behaviors?

2.   Divide into two groups, male and female. Discuss how you approach initiating a friendship or relationship? How do you pursue a new friendship or relationship? Are these approaches gender-related? Are such approaches completely individual or can some generalities be drawn about the differences between males and females in this area?

3.   List (minimum of 10) shared values which you consider most important in an intimate relationship. Gather in small groups to compare lists. Are some values cited over and over again?

4.   Divide into three or four groups. Then present a type of "game playing" in a relationship. There will be two key players (who "game play") and one or more ancillary players who simply observe or who may participate in the "game." When all scenes are completed, have a discussion on why each kind of "game playing" was ineffective. What could have been done instead to resolve the conflict?

5.   List some of the many ways men are socially conditioned differently from women in our culture. Discuss whether all or many of these differences are <u>truly significant</u> or are they "smoke screens?"

6.   List books or movies of the last 10 years where they felt the two leading characters shared a truly, affirming intimate relationship. Supporting statements are necessary. Some examples might be:

-    <u>Out of Africa</u> - book/film
-    <u>The Bridges of Madison County</u> - book/film
-    <u>The Prince of Tides</u> - book/film.

7.   In this society it is said that in most types of relationships, men tend to be the withdrawers. Is this an unfair social expectation placed on men's responses or is there much truth to the "accusation?" Discuss viewpoints. Any recent books or movies that seem to support this view?

8.   Read the short poem by the poet John Ciardi entitled "The Plea." After a few minutes to analyze the poem, be prepared to discuss what the poet/speaker effectively is saying to his partner. What is the conflict which seems to be at work here?

9.   In the 80's movie, "Terms of Endearment," the focus of the movie centers around the mother-daughter relationship. Watch a clip from the movie. In small groups, discuss a core dynamic that seems to be at play between the mother and daughter in this movie. Does this dynamic play itself out in most present-day mother-daughter relationships? What other "roles" or positions do mothers and daughters assume/play out, do you feel? Are they basically healthy or unhealthy?

TEST QUESTIONS

<u>Multiple Choice</u>

9.1   According to Schutz, humans have three fundamental needs. They are:

     a.   inclusion, control and affirmation
  * b.   inclusion, control and affection
     c.   control, affection and security
     d.   affection, inclusion and self-esteem
     e.   none of the above

9.2   Complementary relationships are those in which:

* a.   one partner supplies what the other lacks.
  b.   both partners fulfill all the other's needs.
  c.   one partner has more control in the relationship than the other partner.
  d.   each partner gives the other continuous praise.
  e.   more than one of the above

9.3   Continually weighing the relative rewards and costs of a relationship describes which theory?

  a.   complementary and symmetrical unions theory
  b.   Maslow's affection needs theory
  c.   Maslow's self-actualization needs theory
  d.   Berlo's social enhancement theory
* e.   Thibaut and Kelley's social exchange theory.

9.4   According to Knapp, the second stage in the development of a relationship is:

* a.   experimenting.
  b.   initiating.
  c.   intensifying.
  d.   bonding.
  e.   integrating.

9.5   The first stage in a couple's "dialectic tension" is:

  a.   novelty and predictability.
  b.   openness and closedness.
  c.   autonomy and predictability.
* d.   autonomy and connection.
  e.   more than one of the above

9.6   According to Steve Duck, humans:

  a.   cannot fully disclose to other humans.
  b.   develop intimate relationships only rarely.
* c.   filter information over a period of time to discover others who match them in attitudes and personality.
  d.   do not expect to develop truly intimate relationships.
  e.   tend to be shallow and superficial in developing relationships.

9.7   People seek close unions because of:

      a.   insecurity and mistrust.
      b.   the need to maintain privacy.
      c.   the fear of being alone.
* d.   interpersonal needs.
      e.   the need of safety in numbers.

9.8   The need to interact with others and to be part of their group is:

      a.   intimacy.
* b.   inclusion.
      c.   affirmation.
      d.   reciprocal needs.
      e.   none of the above

9.9   The amount of fondness or tender feelings you have for others or want them to have for you is termed:

      a.   intimacy.
* b.   affection.
      c.   union.
      d.   inclusion.
      e.   relational space.

9.10   Mark Knapp has divided relationship stages into two categories. They are:

* a.   development and disintegration
      b.   casual and close
      c.   tentative and stable
      d.   hit and miss
      e.   bonding and terminating

9.11   The most satisfied couples in a union recognize and emphasize the three elements of:

      a.   friendship, romantic and sexual attraction.
      b.   compatibility, romantic and sexual attraction.
* c.   shared values, friendship & compatibility.
      d.   shared values, compatibility and romantic attraction.
      e.   shared values, romantic attraction and friendship.

9.12   A right-brain activity characterized by feelings of euphoria is called:

      a.   sexual attraction.
* b.   romantic attraction or limerance.
      c.   friendship.
      d.   conflict.
      e.   none of the above

9.13   An expressed struggle between at least two independent parties who perceive incompatible goals, scare rewards, and interference from the other party in achieving their goals describes:

      a.   interpersonal needs.
      b.   social exchange theory.
      c.   dialectic.
* d.   conflict.
      e.   gunny-sacking.

9.14   Which of the following is not a destructive approach to resolving conflict in close relationships?

      a.   aggression
      b.   avoidance
      c.   blaming
      d.   playing games
* e.   negotiating

9.15   An effective way to handle conflict is to:

      a.   see the problem from the other point of view.
      b.   listen carefully.
      c.   seek mutual problem solving.
      d.   seek to settle the conflict on the idea level.
* e.   all of the above

9.16   The stage of relationship disintegration where withdrawing occurs is termed:

      a.   differentiating.
      b.   circumscribing.
      c.   stagnating.
* d.   avoiding.
      e.   terminating.

9.17   Cody found that:

   a.   relationships rarely break up abruptly.
* b.   the closer the relationship, the greater was the obligation of the one ending it to justify such a step.
   c.   partners will not sever the relationship if it was an intimate one.
   d.   usually, both partners will move to end the relationship.
   e.   even in intimate relationships, both partners frequently move in and out of the intimacy based on various factors.

9.18   The best intimate relationships:

   a.   demand work.
   b.   rarely happen because of "luck."
   c.   require self-disclosure.
   d.   bring immense satisfaction and happiness.
* e.   all of the above

9.19   The difference between a close friendship and a superficial friendship is that close friends:

   a.   show emotional support.
   b.   trust one another.
   c.   seek to keep a certain distance.
   d.   volunteer to assist when there is a need.
* e.   two or more of the above

9.20   Some friendships end because:

   a.   there has been a serious falling out.
   b.   the individuals involved simply lost interest.
   c.   one may have changed, the other stayed the same.
   d.   people move away and find it difficult to stay in touch.
* e.   all of the above

True or False

9.1   Intimate relationships can be described as those that last over a long period of time, involve a high degree of intensity and a high degree of self-disclosure and contain strong affection.

* a.   true
   b.   false

9.2   Most intimate relationships take a long time to develop and mature.

    * a.   true
      b.   false

9.3   Most couples in American society base their relationships more on physical looks than they do on similar attitudes.

      a.   true
    * b.   false

9.4   "Control" refers to the need to interact with others and be part of their group.

      a.   true
    * b.   false

9.5   A symmetrical relationship is one in which one partner supplies what the other lacks.

      a.   true
    * b.   false

9.6   To be classified as an "intimate union," a relationship must be romantic and/or sexual.

      a.   true
    * b.   false

9.7   Close relationships for most people are the most important form of interpersonal communication in their lives.

    * a.   true
      b.   false

9.8   People rarely, if ever, reveal <u>everything</u> they believe, think, and feel to another human.

    * a.   true
      b.   false

9.9   Most people have more than ten friends that they would qualify as "intimates" or close friends.

      a.   true
    * b.   false

9.10   The need for "control" is each person's need to shape the behavior of others.

    * a.   true
      b.   false

9.11   As a rule, all people share the same drives, needs and motivations.

      a.   true
    * b.   false

9.12   Rewards are what keep a relationship going.

    * a.   true
      b.   false

9.13   Some people will stay in a close union only if the rewards exceed the cost.

    * a.   true
      b.   false

9.14   Love at first sight or instant attraction between two people occurs occasionally, but is not the norm.

    * a.   true
      b.   false

9.15   Mark Knapp states that "initiating" is the first step in the disintegration of a close relationship.

      a.   true
    * b.   false

9.16   A union becomes "bonded" when a pair formalizes their union, usually by way of a contract.

    * a.   true
      b.   false

9.17   The methods described in the chapter for dealing with conflict invariably work when practiced on a regular basis.

      a.   true
    * b.   false

9.18   Friendships, unlike many close unions, are voluntary.

    * a.   true
       b.   false

9.19   True friends or intimates don't argue or get involved in deep conflict.

       a.   true
    * b.   false

9.20   You are fortunate indeed if you have one friend who has always been there for you.

    * a.   true
       b.   false

Short Essays

9.1   Please describe how intimate or close relationships are fundamentally different from superficial friendships.

9.2   While opposites may be attracted to each other in the beginning of a relationship, the partners do not always do well after they have been together for a while. Please explain why this could happen.

9.3   Think of your best friend. Why do you consider this person your "best friend?" Would he/she consider you to be his/her "best friend" also? Why or why not?

9.4   Explain why sexual attraction should not be the most important element in a relationship.

9.5   How is "blaming" an immature response to conflict resolution? Does blaming begin in early childhood? Explain.

9.6   Write about an instance when you did an admirable job of resolving a conflict. What was the nature of the conflict? Who was involved? How did you manage and then resolve the conflict? Be as detailed as possible.

9.7   "Friendship always benefits; love sometimes injures."—Seneca. Write a paragraph/essay supporting or disputing this statement.

9.8   What function does romance (or limerance) play in an intimate relationship? What can be a pitfall? Why is romantic attraction so emphasized in this culture?

9.9   Describe a destructive form of conflict in a parent-child relationship. What makes this form of conflict so destructive?

9.10   Are shared values really so important in a close relationship? How are shared values often "the tie that binds?" Or is this just a cliche? Explain in some detail.

CHAPTER 10

FAMILY INTERPERSONAL COMMUNICATION

CHAPTER SYNOPSIS

A primary source for developing and maintaining interpersonal relationships is the family. The family as a **system** provides a launching pad for the development of relationships and a support system that continues to grow and change throughout life.

A variety of **family communication functions** emerge as families grow and change. Families offer social **support** to one another as well as serving as the main source for **identity formation**. Communication within families also greatly influences self-concept and **value formation**.

Learning about family **roles**, **rules**, and **interaction patterns** provides important insights into family relationships. Roles are socially determined sets of expected, patterned behaviors individuals assume as they occupy a position in the family. Family role functions pivot on role expectations—the unwritten rules—that families (and society) have established for men and women.

While communication rules are not limited to role expectations, they help families maintain a sense of stability and predictability. Family communication rules also influence **interaction patterns**. **Family communication networks** establish certain rule patterns as well.

Learning about roles, rules and interaction patterns provides important insights into family relationships. However, as human beings, families argue, disagree, and fight. Managing, rather than avoiding, conflict can lead to greater satisfaction with family life. If people can look at conflict situations as opportunities for growth in learning and understanding, they'll probably find they experience more satisfaction from their family relationships.

Lastly, it is not surprising that the "typical" family is not so typical anymore. **Single-parent families**, **step-families**, and families headed by **same-sex couples** often face unique communication problems. As research continues, we will find more documentation and insights into what used to be considered the not-so-typical family.

CHAPTER OUTLINE

I. The Family System
    A.   Subsystems
    B.   Open System
        1.   Internal Influences
        2.   External Influences

II. Functions of Family Communication
    A.   Support
        1.   Feeling of Intimacy
    B.   Personality and Identity
        1.   Self-Concept
    C.   Value Formation
    D.   Everyday Life

III. Family Roles, Rules, and Interaction Patterns
    A.   Roles
        1.   Gender and Roles
    B.   Rules
        1.   Explicit
        2.   Unwritten
        3.   Stability and Predictability
    C.   Interaction Patterns
        1.   Family-of-Origin Influences
        2.   Networks
            a.   Chain
            b.   "Y"
            c.   Wheel
            d.   All-Channel

IV. Conflict: Unavoidable, Inevitable, and Manageable
    A.   Struggle
    B.   Disagreement
    C.   Managing Conflict Constructively
        1.   Attack the Issue
        2.   Stick to One Issue
        3.   Strive for Win-Win Situation
        4.   Listen and Confront Actively

5. Take Responsibility
6. Direct and Specific Language
7. Use Humor for Relief

V. The Typical Family is Not So Typical
   A. Single-Parent Families
   B. Step-Families
   C. Same-Sex Couples
   D. Communication Consequences

VI. Communicating Competently in Families

TEACHING OBJECTIVES

▸ To describe the family as part of a communication system.

▸ To explore the functions of communication in a family.

▸ To delineate the variety of ways in which rules govern communication behaviors in families.

▸ To explore patterns of family interaction.

▸ To illustrate the role of conflict in families and steps in managing conflict.

▸ To explore communication issues that face "nontraditional" families.

TOPICS FOR STUDENT JOURNAL ENTRIES OR ESSAY ASSIGNMENTS:

1. Draw a diagram of your family communication patterns. This diagram should reveal the nature of communication between all family members. For example, is the communication between siblings always conflict laden or open? Along with reflecting on communication issues, the diagram could reflect roles, status, or relationships. Write about how this diagram reflects your family's communication.

2. Recall a happy occasion in your family. This could be a particular holiday, party, family tradition, etc. Who was there? What was happening? If your feelings regarding this event are generally good, something must have gone right in the communication events. Based on your readings in this chapter, what communication issues were effective in this happy occasion? Why was communication effective in this circumstance?

3. Write about the members of your immediate family. Identify their roles within the family. What character traits are associated with these roles? What behaviors shape these

roles within your family? Where do you fit? What role(s) do you play? What are your traits and behaviors which accompany these roles?

4.   Think of a family relationship in which you want communication to improve. For example, it could be you and your mother, your cousin, step-father, sibling, etc. What is the nature of communication in that relationship now? What do you want to change? How could you improve communication in this relationship? What is your goal for communication in this relationship?

IN-CLASS ACTIVITIES FOR STUDENTS:

1.   Discuss your family's unwritten rules. For example, what topics are never discussed? What issues are considered private? Are there acceptable and unacceptable behaviors? How do you think these unwritten rules have changed since your parents were growing up? How do you foresee them changing for future generations in your family?

2.   Create an outline for a one-day workshop on "Marriage" or "Family Enrichment" which focuses on family communication as the key topic. Establish goals and criteria for this workshop. What issues would you cover and how would you accomplish this?

3.   Watch a clip from a well-known movie (such as "Guess Who's Coming to Dinner?") in which a family's value system is being challenged by one of it's members. Discuss the interchange occurring in the clip. Are the individual members of the family managing the conflict? How do they manage the conflict specifically?

4.   In the movie, "Ordinary People," a mother harbors bitter resentments relating to the death of her youngest and "favorite" son. Watch a scene from near the conclusion of the movie in which the father and the older son decide they must leave home (and the wife/mother) because to stay would destroy them all.

Discuss how the father and son in the movie have had to set a "bottom line" with the mother's behaviors to preserve their own sense of dignity and well-being.

5.   What are some "games" some fathers and sons "play" with one another? What are some "games" some mothers and daughters "play" with one another? Why does such game-playing occur?

6.   In small groups of four or five individuals, discuss how the "typical" family is not so typical anymore. In what ways are non-traditional families non-traditional? Does this help or hinder the individuals making up these non-traditional families? In what ways are the members positively or negatively impacted?

7.   Draw a three-generational family tree to share with the rest of the class. How many class members come from traditional families? How many come from a non-traditional family?

TEST QUESTIONS

<u>Multiple Choice</u>

10.1   "In my family a college education is of utmost importance. My parents constantly made references to our future goals of attending college." This quote depicts the family function known as:

   a.   family tradition.
   b.   support.
   c.   identity formation.
   d.   getting ahead.
 * e.   value formation.

10.2   _____ are socially determined sets of expected, patterned behaviors that individuals assume as they occupy a position in the family.

   a.   Rules
 * b.   Roles
   c.   Identities
   d.   Communication patterns
   e.   Self-expectations

10.3   Shimanoff, (1980) suggests that _____ "may function to regulate, interpret, evaluate, justify, correct, predict, and explain behavior."

 * a.   rules
   b.   roles
   c.   identities
   d.   communication patterns
   e.   self-expectations

10.4   A family communication pattern which is characteristic of families with a strong decision-making, central figure in the middle is the:

   a.   all-channel network.
   b.   chain network.
 * c.   wheel pattern.
   d.   Y network.
   e.   octagon pattern.

10.5 _____ reflect the experiences one has growing up in the family (or families) and is considered to be the earliest and most powerful influence on one's personality.

    a.   Multigenerational transmissions
    b.   Cultural heritages
    c.   Communication rules
* d.   Family-of-origin influences
    e.   Interaction patterns

10.6 In a study conducted by Dolores Curran to identify traits typical of a healthy family, the most highly rated quality was:

    a.   conflict resolution.
    b.   acceptance of the individual.
    c.   role identification.
* d.   the ability to communicate.
    e.   the interdependence of the family members.

10.7 According to Webster's dictionary, "a group of persons of common ancestry; a group of individuals living under one roof and under one head; a social group composed of children and their parents" is defined as a:

    a.   subsystem.
    b.   unit.
* c.   family.
    d.   family network.
    e.   multigenerational chain.

10.8 Which of the following is a family communication function?

    a.   offering support in a number of ways
    b.   providing identity formation
    c.   influencing value formation
    d.   helping to deal with the practical events of everyday life
* e.   all of the above

10.9 When it comes to sex role expectations in many traditional families:

    a.   the traditional view is ideal.
    b.   the contemporary view is best.
* c.   whatever works in the individual family to help in healthy functioning is best.
    d.   defined "rules" must be imposed.
    e.   none of the above

10.10   Most often, family members discover the "rules" of their family when they:

      a.   frequently sit down together and "set down" rules.
      b.   are directly told what is or is not acceptable.
      c.   reflect on what works in other families.
  * d.   partake in and observe interaction episodes within their own families.
      e.   use the "hit or miss" method of guesswork.

10.11   Rules serve many functions in the family system:

      a.   they help families maintain a sense of stability and predictability.
      b.   they guide family members' behavior.
      c.   they help to avoid chaos.
      d.   they pattern behavior living outside the family unit.
  * e.   all of the above

10.12   The interaction patterns as to who talks to whom and about what is known as:

  * a.   family communication network.
      b.   family rules.
      c.   family conflict modality.
      d.   role identity.
      e.   none of the above

10.13   A family communication pattern in which all family members freely exchange messages with each other is known as the:

      a.   chain network.
  * b.   all-channel network.
      c.   Y communication network.
      d.   wheel pattern.
      e.   ABC - Talk to me pattern.

10.14   Typically, conflict in families emerge when:

      a.   one member is verbally or physically abusive to one or more other members of the family.
      b.   the costs outweigh the rewards.
      c.   the pain inflicted outweighs the happiness engendered.
      d.   there are misunderstood or unfulfilled role expectations.
  * e.   two or more of the above

10.15   In "constructive conflict," we learn to:

      a.   use humor, not ridicule.
      b.   stick to one issue at a time.
      c.   strive for a win-win situation.
      d.   listen and confront actively.
 * e.   two or more of the above

10.16   A family consisting of two adults and the children of one or both of them is called a:

      a.   single-parent family.
      b.   same-sex headed family.
 * c.   step-family.
      d.   homogeneous unit.
      e.   none of the above

10.17   A communication consequence of a same-sex family relationship is:

      a.   difficulty in talking to their children about their choices in relationships.
      b.   little social support.
      c.   feelings of isolation.
      d.   difficulty in talking about their lifestyle.
 * e.   two or more of the above

10.18   When the family is an "open system,":

 * a.   the unit is influenced by and influences its external environment.
      b.   it fends off all external pressures.
      c.   it is less pressured by religious and/or social organizations.
      d.   it is not so susceptible to cultural norms.
      e.   all of the above

10.19   "Value formation" occurs in a family when:

      a.   parents instill the values they experienced in their own families of origin.
      b.   individual accomplishments and successes are celebrated.
      c.   individual goals are discussed and encouraged, whether those goals are necessarily desirable or not.
      d.   particular educational activities are practiced such as a daily family "reading hour."
 * e.   all of the above

10.20   Some influences on sex role development other than the family unit are:

      a.   religious groups.
      b.   social groups.
      c.   interactions with peer groups.
      d.   the media.
   * e.   all of the above

True or False

10.1   If we consider the family system as a whole unit, then there are parts or extensions of the family that are called subsystems.

   * a.   true
      b.   false

10.2   In families where communication is healthy, conflict is absent.

      a.   true
   * b.   false

10.3   Failure to understand the "rules" of our families often leads to misunderstanding, frustration, and conflict.

   * a.   true
      b.   false

10.4   The film "Mr. Mom" provides a prime example of gender-role confusion.

   * a.   true
      b.   false

10.5   There is very little room for distortion of family communication in the <u>chain</u> network.

      a.   true
   * b.   false

10.6   The "family system" approach looks at the family as an entire unit, rather than as the sum of its parts."

   * a.   true
      b.   false

10.7   As a family unit grows larger, the interpersonal subsystems become more complex.

     * a.   true
       b.   false

10.8   The family is essentially a closed unit.

       a.   true
     * b.   false

10.9   One of the characteristics of a family unit is that the family members tend to share the same talents and exact experiences.

       a.   true
     * b.   false

10.10   Sex role development is not influenced by family of origin: outside influences foster or inhibit sex role development.

       a.   true
     * b.   false

10.11   In families where communication patterns are considered healthy, individuals are allowed to be flexible in their roles.

     * a.   true
       b.   false

10.12   Clear expectations regarding role behaviors make for successful family communication.

     * a.   true
       b.   false

10.13   Role expectations govern sex role behaviors.

       a.   true
     * b.   false

10.14   According to Buchner and Eisenberg, "family-of-origin" influences reflect the experiences one has growing up in the family (or families) and are the earliest and most powerful influences on one's personality.

     * a.   true
       b.   false

10.15 Racial, ethnic or cultural patterns have little or no influence on family interaction patterns.

      a.   true
* b.   false

10.16 Conflict and stress in families could be eliminated entirely if people followed suggestions for coping with stress and managing conflict.

      a.   true
* b.   false

10.17 "The happy family knows it can't always be happy."

* a.   true
      b.   false

10.18 In conflict management, a guideline is to attack the issue, not the person.

* a.   true
      b.   false

10.19 Today, the single-parent family population makes up one-half of all families with children.

      a.   true
* b.   false

10.20 Role-related conflicts do not seem to emerge as frequently in same-sex relationships as they do in heterosexual relationships.

* a.   true
      b.   false

10.21 Same-sex couples with children find themselves facing issues similar to those of heterosexual couples with children.

* a.   true
      b.   false

Short Essays

10.1 List and describe three of the suggested guidelines for managing conflict constructively.

10.2   Compare and contrast the communication related issues that affect single-parent and step-parent families. How do these differ from what used to be considered "traditional" or "typical" family communication issues?

10.3   In her book, <u>The Dance of Intimacy</u>, Harriet Goldhor Lerner states: "Family connectedness, even when these relationships are anxious and difficult, is a necessary prerequisite to conducting one's own intimate relationships free from serious symptoms over time and free from excessive anxiety and reactivity." Respond in some detail to this statement.

10.4   Discuss how a particular "rule" in your family of origin either helped or hindered your later interaction with others.

10.5   Describe the family from a systems perspective.

10.6   Harriet Goldhor Lerner has stated: "We cannot navigate clearly within a relationship unless we can live without it." Explain how this concept relates to family connectedness and the task of the individual to find some separateness beyond the family construct.

10.7   Explain the "chain network" concept as it applies to family interpersonal communication.

10.8   One of the chapter headings is entitled "The Typical Family is NOT so Typical." What does <u>this</u> statement mean?

10.9   What are 2-3 "unwritten" rules in your present family situation? Do you wish these unwritten rules were more explicit? Explain your responses.

10.10   Why is "sticking to one issue at a time" so important in constructive conflict resolution?

CHAPTER 11

PROFESSIONAL RELATIONSHIPS

CHAPTER SYNOPSIS

Professional interpersonal relationships are often different than other kinds. For one reason, workers don't have the kind of trust they might have with intimates. This, in turn, often makes conflict more difficult to deal with. Other factors that affect a professional environment are communication **climates**, **roles** people are expected to play and the **formal** and **informal** rules they have to follow.

Leaders wield strong influence in the workplace. Their styles can be **autocratic**, **bureaucratic**, **persuasive** and **participative**. Leaders initiate the downward flow of messages employees receive. Sometimes this information is inadequate or gets distorted and causes serious communication problems. Upward communication—the kind employees send to superiors—is less frequent but carries its own set of potential problems. Distortion sometimes occurs when employees relay only messages they think superiors want to hear. Horizontal communication is the flow of messages between employees with equal status. A variant of this kind of communication is cross-channel communication—the transferring of messages between members of segments within an institution.

Employees talking to customers is another vital communication channel. In a market-driven economy, customer service becomes a crucial component for successful companies. The care and feeding of customers has been one of the most important functions of businesses today.

A final form of professional communication is the grapevine—the informal channel that carries messages throughout an organization. Grapevines have pluses and minuses. Bosses and employees are well served when they know what these are. Messages relayed through the grapevine are usually fast, generally accurate and provide a gauge for employee morale. On the negative side, grapevine messages usually contain some errors and often transmit rumors.

A final important kind of organizational communication is the interview. Interviews can range from the job interview to employee evaluations to an information gathering session. All three types demand special skills to be effective.

CHAPTER OUTLINE

I.   Why Work Relationships are Different from Other Kinds
      A.   Communication Climate
      B.   Roles in the Workplace
      C.   Rules

II.   Leaders' Styles in an Organization
      A.   Autocratic
      B.   Bureaucratic
      C.   Persuasive
      D.   Participative

III.   Communication Channels
    A.   Downward Communication
    B.   Upward
    C.   Horizontal
    D.   Employee Communication to Customers
    E.   The Grapevine

IV.   Interviews
    A.   The Job Interview
        1.   The Opening of the Interview
        2.   The Middle
        3.   The Ending
    B.   The Employee Evaluation Interview
        1.   For the Supervisor
        2.   For the One Being Evaluated
    C.   The Information Gathering Interview

TEACHING OBJECTIVES

▸   To explore the special interpersonal communication skills necessary in the professional workplace.

▸   To describe communication patterns that characterize managers and employees.

▸   To explicate four leadership styles and the communication behaviors that accompany each.

▸   To explore both formal and informal lines and uses of communication in an organization.

TOPICS FOR STUDENT JOURNAL ENTRIES OR ESSAY ASSIGNMENTS:

1.   Describe one effective and one ineffective meeting you have attended. What made them effective or ineffective? What communication aspects contributed to the effectiveness or ineffectiveness of the meeting?

2.   Observe the communication patterns of a professional relationship you are in or one with which you are familiar. What are the patterns you observe over a day? What is the status of the communication? Is it upward, downward, or horizontal most often?

3.   Using the same relationship you observed in Journal #2, diagram the communication networks and explain your diagram. Be sure to include key terms noted in the text.

4.   Compare and contrast a personal and a professional relationship you are in. How is communication similar? How does communication differ? What about a professional relationship which is **also** personal. How does communication differ in this instance?

IN-CLASS ACTIVITIES FOR STUDENTS:

1.   Conduct a mock interview with some people as interviewers, some as interviewees, and some as observers. Change roles periodically so everyone will have the opportunity to play each role. Script typical interview questions for different types of jobs. Observers should critique content as well as delivery style.

2.   Divide into interviewers and interviewees. In pairs, practice conducting a successful employment interview with each other. Allow time for feedback with each other.

3.   As a written exercise, identify your favorite interviewer on television. Discuss what techniques make this person effective as an interviewer.

4.   Divide into four groups. Each group should make up a short 2-3 minute skit which demonstrates how the "organizational grapevine" can work—for good or ill. Allow 15 minutes to set up the skits.

At the conclusion of each skit, assess what occurred in each skit and whether, in each instance, a probable negative or positive result would occur.

5.   Divide into 3 or 4 groups. Then select a current or fairly recent world leader (i.e. former President Clinton, Margaret Thatcher, President George W. Bush, Winston Churchill) and discuss what leadership style that individual seemed to practice.

List specific characteristics of that person's leadership style to back up their position.

6.   Provide a list of reasons why supervisor-employee relations are often so strained? Write the list on the board. (List up to 8) One by one, provide a viable solution to each negative interaction.

TEST QUESTIONS

<u>Multiple Choice</u>

11.1   Communication climate refers to:

      a.   predominant weather pattern of an organization's location.
      b.   the relationship between boss and employees.
  * c.   the interpersonal tone in an organization.
      d.   the expectations members have of their superiors.
      e.   none of the above

11.2   Redding maintains that communication climate is largely a product of employee perceptions. He suggests five elements that help account for a positive communication climate. Four of the five are: support from superiors, influence in decision-making, trust of messages from colleagues and the candor of messages. Which is the fifth element?

      a.   how much influence employees have in salary negotiations
      b.   how educated each employee is in his or her particular job
  * c.   the clarity of performance goals
      d.   insurance and retirement benefits
      e.   job security

11.3   Roles can be described as:

  * a.   recurring behavioral patterns that individuals engage in within a social system.
      b.   the way people communicate with each other inter-personally in an office.
      c.   supervisors only.
      d.   employees only.
      e.   the expectations that supervisors have of employees.

11.4   Organization rules are:

      a.   requirements listed in a job manual.
      b.   guidelines about ways to dress and behave in an organization.
      c.   the usually unwritten and unspoken understandings about appropriate ways to interact with others in an organization.
      d.   guidelines included in an employee's evaluation form.
  * e.   more than one of the above

11.5   One who leads primarily by command and force of personality can be described as what kind of leader?

      a.   persuasive
      b.   laissez-faire
      c.   charismatic
   * d.   autocratic
      e.   judgmental

11.6   Co-workers normally don't develop the kind of solid relationship that occurs between intimates or good friends because:

      a.   they don't get to choose who they want to work with.
      b.   they don't get to choose who does business with their company or organization.
      c.   they must assume a "role" which they may or may not feel comfortable with.
      d.   they must abide by the "rules" of the workplace which they may or may not feel comfortable with.
   * e.   all of the above

11.7   One of the following is <u>not</u> an element that characterizes an effective supervisor:

      a.   she talks easily to her staff
      b.   she is an excellent listener
   * c.   she commands respect and can demand what she wants
      d.   she is sensitive to the needs of employees
      e.   she can disseminate information readily

11.8   A quality of a top boss is that she:

      a.   praises subordinates.
      b.   shows trust.
      c.   offers warmth.
      d.   allows for the freedom to disagree.
   * e.   two or more of the above

11.9   "Downward communication" is often ineffective because:

      a.   information is inadequate.
      b.   methods of transferring the information are inadequate.
      c.   information gets distorted as it is filtered downward.
      d.   messages frequently follow a pattern of dominance-submission.
   * e.   all of the above

11.10 Pace and Boren describe the inaccurate filtering of downward messages as:

      a.   downward communication.
* b.   serial reproduction.
      c.   horizontal communication.
      d.   cross channel communication.
      e.   none of the above

11.11 The term "upward communication" refers to:

* a.   messages subordinates relay to supervisors.
      b.   messages aimed at intensifying and augmenting employee self-esteem.
      c.   messages among managers and leaders who represent the "upper" ranks of the organization.
      d.   messages among the upwardly mobile in an organization or group.
      e.   messages aimed at providing only accurate, clear information.

11.12 Communication between segments within an organization is termed:

      a.   upward communication.
      b.   downward communication.
* c.   cross-channel communication.
      d.   participate communication.
      e.   reasoned communication.

11.13 "The organizational grapevine" is characterized as:

      a.   fast.
      b.   transmits rumors.
      c.   generally accurate.
      d.   providing a gauge of employee sentiment.
* e.   two or more of the above

11.14 A disadvantage of the "organizational grapevine" is that it:

      a.   transmits inaccurate or distorted messages.
      b.   agitates people and can destroy a company.
      c.   disrupts work.
      d.   is not professional in approach.
* e.   two or more of the above

11.15   In preparing for a successful job interview, the applicant needs to:

   * a.   prepare in advance.
     b.   be aggressive and pushy, if necessary.
     c.   dress comfortably and as you normally would look day-to-day.
     d.   be realistic and not expect too much.
     e.   avoid asking many questions; it gives the impression you don't know much about the company.

11.16   A form of interview in which an employer sits down with an employee to provide feedback on work performance is described as:

     a.   routine job interview.
   * b.   evaluation interview.
     c.   information-gathering interview.
     d.   interviewer-applicant interview.
     e.   informal feedback interview.

11.17   A hallmark of a positive employee evaluation interview is that it:

     a.   seeks to instill confidence and a sense of good will about the job.
     b.   demonstrates purpose and provides specific feedback.
     c.   provides concrete ways to improve job performance.
     d.   ends on a positive note.
   * e.   all of the above

11.18   Job and information-gathering interviews:

   * a.   don't assume that the participants have already established a relationship.
     b.   assume the participants have already established a relationship.
     c.   usually prove fruitful; you get the job.
     d.   are tedious and time-consuming and usually a waste of time.
     e.   require limited personal contact.

11.19   For a person being interviewed, it is best to:

     a.   start with a positive attitude.
     b.   greet the interviewer in a warm way.
     c.   listen carefully to the feedback/responses.
     d.   ask appropriate questions to ascertain the information you need.
   * e.   all of the above

11.20   During an interview, a **leading** question is one in which:

      a.   the interviewer is not looking for a desired answer.
      b.   the interviewer tries to embarrass the applicant.
      c.   the interviewer wants to hear **one** answer.
      d.   the question is impossible to answer.
  * e.   the applicant is asked personal questions.

True or False

11.1   Communication climate largely affects non-supervisors but rarely, if ever, does it impact supervisors.

      a.   true
  * b.   false

11.2   For a vice president of a company, climate is even more important than the structure or context of the company.

  * a.   true
      b.   false

11.3   A formal role is one a company assigns to an employee.

  * a.   true
      b.   false

11.4   Someone who is a nurturer and supporter is assuming an informal role in a company.

  * a.   true
      b.   false

11.5   The breaking of informal rules in an organization can lead to losing one's job.

  * a.   true
      b.   false

11.6   According to Goldhaber, the most important factor in job satisfaction for employees is salary.

      a.   true
  * b.   false

11.7   A supervisor should never use an autocratic style with employees.

      a.   true
* b.   false

11.8   Co-workers normally don't develop the kind of bond that allows them to trust as do intimates or good friends.

* a.   true
      b.   false

11.9   A bureaucratic leader is one who relies on a set of rules.

* a.   true
      b.   false

11.10   A participative leader is one who tries to motivate followers rather than tell them what to do.

      a.   true
* b.   false

11.11   A disadvantage of the participative leader approach is that it demands a clear sense of direction.

      a.   true
* b.   false

11.12   The best leadership style depends on the ability of the leader, the employees themselves, and the situation.

* a.   true
      b.   false

11.13   If a group is self-motivated and experienced, its members might do better with a persuasive or participative leader.

* a.   true
      b.   false

11.14   "Downward communication" refers to messages traveling from leaders to subordinates.

* a.   true
      b.   false

11.15   "Serial reproduction" is the flow of messages among employees who have equal status within an organization.

        a.   true
    * b.   false

11.16   In employee-customer relations, the customer is always right.

    * a.   true
        b.   false

11.17   The "organizational grapevine" is the formal channel that carries messages from one person to another.

        a.   true
    * b.   false

11.18   As a rule, the resumé should be one page.

    * a.   true
        b.   false

Short Essays

11.1   Please describe the communication climate in an organization. Then discuss how communication climate affects employee morale.

11.2   Chapter 11, deals with informal and formal roles in an organization. Please explain why a supervisor needs to be aware of both kinds of roles when dealing with employees during a performance evaluation.

11.3   Discuss the leadership style you prefer to work under and why. Try to avoid superficial responses.

11.4   Discuss a leadership style you would find extremely difficult to work under. Why couldn't you adapt to that leadership style? Would you be willing to adapt if it were for the sake of a position that was greatly important to you?

11.5   Provide an example of how the "organizational grapevine" proved advantageous in a particular work situation. Be specific.

11.6   Think of a time when you had a "bad" job interview. What factors made it seem to be a "bad" interview? What could/should you have done to make it a "good" interview experience?

11.7   List some techniques successful companies use in relating to their customers.

11.8   List and discuss four suggestions provided in the chapter for conducting successful meetings in small groups.

11.9   Discuss three techniques a supervisor can use to help insure a productive employee evaluation interview.

CHAPTER 12

INTERPERSONAL COMMUNICATION IN THE GLOBAL VILLAGE: ISSUES OF CULTURE AND GENDER

CHAPTER SYNOPSIS

We live in a multicultural world. When we communicate with someone of a different cultural background than our own, we are engaging in **interpersonal communication**. To a certain extent, interpersonal and intercultural communication are alike. In both, the underlying communication processes are the same. The two 'forms' of communication are not different in kind, only in degree. Intercultural communication adds the unique aspect of culturally different backgrounds of interactants and all the variables this brings into play in communication encounters.

Even in the best of circumstances, a degree of **communication dissonance** occurs in intercultural encounters. This dissonance or **communication mismatch** can take place at three levels: language and nonverbal behavior; functions of communication; and cultural understanding.

Cross-cultural, multicultural and **intercultural** are terms describing distinctly different ideas. It is important to understand the difference between these ideas because these terms are sometimes used interchangeably and unfortunately incorrectly. Marshall McLuhan has described the world as a "global village" where we have increasingly come into contact with people who are culturally different. With this ever-increasing cultural contact, our ability to develop interpersonal relationships with others who are culturally different depends on a combination of interpersonal and intercultural skills.

To improve our intercultural skills, it is important to understand what constitutes culture. Additionally, it is necessary to recognize that a culture consists of many co-cultures. The diversity of co-cultures in a given society include ethnic groups, the disabled, age, gender orientation, and religion among others.

Cultures vary along two main variables—(1) **individualism** and **collectivism**, and (2) **high-** and **low-context**. Individualistic cultures place emphasis on individual goals while group goals are more important in collectivist cultures. A high-context culture is long-lived and provides a unifying force that is slow to change. Low-context cultures are not significantly unified and can easily be changed and adapted.

As we learn to communicate with people of other cultures, we develop our **intercultural competence**. There are three important components that make-up intercultural competence. These three components are **motivation, knowledge**, and **skills**. Without motivation many people try to avoid communicating with people who are culturally different because it can be difficult. Even if we are highly motivated however, we may still need to acquire knowledge and skills. Knowledge is the awareness and understanding of what we need to do in order to communicate appropriately and effectively with culturally different people. Once we have knowledge, we need to use it and behave in skillful ways.

Unfortunately, even with the best intentions, intercultural communication can go astray. LaRay Barna has identified six **stumbling blocks to intercultural communication**. These include: assumed similarity; language; nonverbal communication; preconceptions and stereotypes; a tendency to evaluate; and, high anxiety.

CHAPTER OUTLINE

I. What is Intercultural Communication
   A. How Intercultural Communication and Interpersonal Communication Differ?
   B. How do Cross-Cultural, Multicultural and Intercultural Differ?
   C. Why Study Intercultural Communication?

II. Understanding Culture and Diversity
   A. What is Culture?
   B. How is Culture Learned?
      1. enculturation
      2. acculturation
   C. What is a Co-Culture?
   D. Cultural Diversity's Many Forms
      1. Gender
      2. Disability
      3. Religion
      4. Age
      5. Gender Orientation or Sexual Preference
      6. Social-Economic Class

III. How Do Cultures Differ?
   A. Individualism-Collectivism
   B. High-Context, Low-Context Cultures

IV.   Six Stumbling Blocks in Intercultural Pathways
    A.   Assumed Similarity
    B.   Language
    C.   Nonverbal Communication
    D.   Preconceptions and Stereotypes
    E.   Tendency to Evaluate
    F.   High Anxiety

V.   Becoming Interculturally Competent
    A.   Motivation
    B.   Knowledge
    C.   Skills, or a Way of Being

TEACHING OBJECTIVES

▸   To explore the similarities and differences between interpersonal and intercultural communication.

▸   To describe the importance of intercultural communication in the global village.

▸   To clarify the difference between intercultural, multicultural and crosscultural issues.

▸   To explain the role of cultural variability and interpersonal/ intercultural communication.

▸   To delineate the skills necessary in developing intercultural competence.

TOPICS FOR STUDENT JOURNAL ENTRIES OR ESSAY ASSIGNMENTS:

1.   Think of some typical cultural stereotypes which you are exposed to. Are these stereotypes a result of local situations or are they nationally recognized? Why do these stereotypes exist? Do you hold these stereotypes? How do these stereotypes influence your behavior or the behavior of those around you?

2.   After reviewing the section of intercultural competency, assess your own level of intercultural competency. After this assessment, write your own goals for becoming more interculturally competent. How will you pursue these goals? How will you make them a part of your daily life?

3.   What is the role of your nationality/heritage on you and your family? Do you practice any cultural traditions or rituals? Does your heritage play a large role in your communication behaviors or values?

4.   Interview someone about a cultural event they have experienced; for example, an event which is laden with cultural traditions would be a wedding or a funeral. What are the traditions involved? How do they reflect the cultural values and norms? If a personal interview is unavailable, do research on a similar event.

IN-CLASS ACTIVITIES FOR STUDENTS:

1.   In small groups, brainstorm the influences of all foreign cultures on your local environment. Some examples might be local cultural events, stores, foreign restaurants, etc. How does your local environment reflect the cultural variety or lack there of?

2.   Split into two groups. List some cultural characteristics or behaviors. For example, one culture may value touch as a high priority whereas the other does not touch at all. One may value the elderly as the core of the culture. Make the list complete enough so the group could act out the culture. As you act out the culture, have the other group try to guess their cultural values, norms and behaviors.

3.   Discuss what seems to be the present-day gender-roles for "the average man" and "the average woman" in the United States. Have these perceived gender-roles stayed pretty much the same since 1970 or do such gender-roles undergo revision every so many years?

4.   According to Harriet G. Lerner in her book on relationships, The Dance of Intimacy, "gender roles being what they are, it is far more common that he distances and she seeks more togetherness—and that daughters, not sons, will struggle harder around issues of caretaking and family responsibility." Is this so? Is this a cross-cultural issue? Discuss in small groups.

5.   As a class, discuss whether our present-day educational system is truly Eurocentric. If so, how has our educational system been built upon and enriched by such a western-centered system? Be specific with ideas. How can we improve it?—By including more Indo-Asian thought and innovations? Would this be practical? Do we need a wider-based system now that our growing national population is much more diverse and multi-cultural than it was 25 years ago?

6.   In small groups, describe (list) some co-cultures in American society. Are they true co-cultures? In what ways? Is this healthy for our country to be so diverse—so full of co-cultures under the umbrella of a central cultural system? Or do we have a central culture? If so, what is it?

7.   How is ethnicity more of an American phenomena? Discuss as a class or in small groups.

TEST QUESTIONS

<u>Multiple Choice</u>

12.1 _____ is the term coined by Marshall McLuhan to describe the impact of technology as perceived in a psychologically shrinking the world.

    a.   Global exchange
* b.   Global village
    c.   Multicultural world
    d.   One world
    e.   Co-cultural technology

12.2 _____ occurs when you interact with someone from a different cultural background from your own.

* a.   Intercultural communication
    b.   International exchange
    c.   Co-culture
    d.   Global warming
    e.   none of the above

12.3 _____ occurs when there is inharmonious or even incongruent communications.

    a.   Communication disorder
* b.   Communication dissonance
    c.   Communication phenomenon
    d.   Communication dysfunction
    e.   Cross-cultural shock

12.4 The anthropological linguist who coined the term "communication mismatch" is:

    a.   Marshall McLuhan.
    b.   Young Yun Kim.
    c.   William B. Gudykurst.
* d.   John Regan.
    e.   none of the above

12.5   The term _____ refers to the shared social experience humans have made to survive in a particular place in their world.

    * a.   culture
       b.   cross-cultural phenomenon
       c.   encounter
       d.   co-dependency
       e.   intracultural harmony

12.6   _____ is a term used to describe group makeup or perspective:

       a.   Cultural
       b.   Co-cultural
    * c.   Multicultural
       d.   Intercultural
       e.   Infracultural

12.7   _____ plays a key role in defining the processes by which people establish, develop and maintain interpersonal relations."

       a.   Culture
       b.   Co-culture
       c.   Cross-cultural phenomenon
       d.   Cultural diversity
    * e.   Communication

12.8   The global village concept is composed of and includes:

       a.   international students.
       b.   studies abroad programs.
       c.   multinational corporations.
       d.   cultural diversity in a multicultural society.
    * e.   all of the above

12.9   "Culture shock" is more likely to happen when people:

       a.   lack knowledge of the host culture.
       b.   have limited experience with travel.
       c.   have limited experience with foreign people or cultures.
       d.   resist personal change.
    * e.   two or more of the above

12.10   According to anthropologist Ina Corrine Brown, culture is defined as:

      a.   refinement.
      b.   high education level.
* c.   a body of common understandings.
      d.   many races, many ethnic groups.
      e.   individual social expression.

12.11   According to the text, "culture is shared and sets the _____ of a group."

      a.   experiences
* b.   boundaries
      c.   conduct
      d.   acts
      e.   norms

12.12   The term _____ refers to subgroups or subcultures within a culture.

      a.   co-culture
      b.   multicultural
      c.   intercultural
      d.   multi-ethnic
* e.   two or more of the above

12.13   "Cultural diversity" includes the areas of:

* a.   disability, religion, age and gender factors.
      b.   facial features and eye color.
      c.   bone structure and body types.
      d.   all of the above
      e.   none of the above

12.14   The ordering pattern referred to as "high- and low-context cultures" was proposed by:

      a.   Larry Samovar.
      b.   W. B. Gudykurst.
* c.   Edward T. Hall.
      d.   Edward Sapir.
      e.   LaRay Barna.

12.15　In essence, _____ are bound by tradition, that shapes behavior and lifestyles.

      a.　ethnic groups
      b.　individualist cultures
      c.　low-context cultures
   * d.　high-context cultures
      e.　individuals

12.16　A major difference affecting communication in high and low context cultures is that:

      a.　verbal messages are much more important in low-context cultures.
      b.　members of high-context cultures perceive low-context people as less attractive and less credible.
      c.　members of high-context cultures are more sensitive to nonverbal behavior and in reading their environment.
      d.　members of high-context cultures expect others to be sensitive to nonverbal messages and therefore speak less than members of low-context cultures.
   * e.　all of the above

12.17　The three components of competence used to look at ways to develop intercultural relationships and to build community are:

      a.　individualism, collectivism and isolationism.
      b.　ethnicity, diversity and culturalism.
   * c.　motivation, knowledge and skills.
      d.　all of the above
      e.　none of the above

12.18　The tendency to judge other cultures as deficient to one's own is termed:

      a.　stereotyping.
   * b.　ethnocentrism.
      c.　multiculturalism.
      d.　discrimination.
      e.　none of the above

12.19　Two approaches to the study of culture are called the "cultural general" and the "cultural _____" approaches.

   * a.　specific
      b.　isolated
      c.　diversified
      d.　oriented
      e.　stereotype

12.20 Although knowledge and motivation are important intercultural components, people also need to have good intercultural _____.

      a.   speech devices
* b.   skills
      c.   ties
      d.   political savvy
      e.   sense

12.21 An important skill for intercultural communication is to:

      a.   know yourself.
      b.   develop sympathy.
      c.   encourage feedback.
      d.   seek commonalities.
* e.   all of the above

12.22 According to LaRay Barna, a possible major stumbling block to intercultural communication is:

* a.   preconceptions and stereotypes.
      b.   visual defects in people.
      c.   being left-handed.
      d.   all of the above
      e.   none of the above

12.23 An example of a high-context culture is:

      a.   Scandinavia.
      b.   United States.
      c.   Canada.
* d.   Japan.
      e.   New Zealand.

12.24 Factors such as word choice, interruption patterns, vocal inflections and language interpretations and misinterpretations all constitute "_____."

      a.   sub-languages
      b.   communication dissonance
* c.   genderlects
      d.   cultural diversity
      e.   ethnocentricity

12.25 _____ culture is culture directly taught to us, is describable, and is passed on to our offspring.

    a.   Co-adaptive
    b.   Covert
* c.   Overt
    d.   Ethnic
    e.   Ethnocentric

True or False

12.1 Life in a society that is culturally diverse (like the United States) requires people to be competent and creative with "people" skills.

* a.   true
    b.   false

12.2 Intercultural communication and interpersonal communication are inherently different and require different processes.

    a.   true
* b.   false

12.3 A degree of dissonance usually occurs in all intercultural exchanges.

* a.   true
    b.   false

12.4 A cross-cultural phenomenon is a phenomenon that appears in a given culture.

    a.   true
* b.   false

12.5 The terms "multicultural" and "intercultural" essentially mean the same thing.

    a.   true
* b.   false

12.6 "Cultural shock" is the feeling of estrangement people feel in visiting another culture.

* a.   true
    b.   false

12.7   Cultural shock occurs naturally.

    * a.   true
       b.   false

12.8   As a "melting pot," America enjoys a harmonious, multicultural society.

       a.   true
    * b.   false

12.9   Culture is both overt and covert.

    * a.   true
       b.   false

12.10   Essentially, people are culturally determined.

    * a.   true
       b.   false

12.11   A simple activity like drinking a cup of tea is a cultural act.

    * a.   true
       b.   false

12.12   Ethnic groups are forms of co-cultures.

    * a.   true
       b.   false

12.13   As a group, attorneys can be defined as a type of co-culture.

    * a.   true
       b.   false

12.14   Ethnicity is solely an American phenomena because of its levels of diversity.

       a.   true
    * b.   false

12.15   The issue of gender is not a factor of cultural diversity.

       a.   true
    * b.   false

12.16 In the area of moral development, men and women make very different decisions in facing moral dilemmas.

   * a.   true
      b.   false

12.17 Religion is always found at the base of social structure and culture.

   * a.   true
      b.   false

12.18 Collectivist cultures value the individuals who make up those cultures and view independence as a virtue.

      a.   true
   * b.   false

12.19 The concept of individualism-collectivism has been recognized as perhaps the most significant dimension of cultural variability.

   * a.   true
      b.   false

12.20 Generally speaking, members of high-context, collectivistic cultures speak indirectly.

   * a.   true
      b.   false

12.21 "People are people." We are all essentially alike.

      a.   true
   * b.   false

12.22 Most nonverbal symbols are culturally specific and therefore vary from culture to culture.

   * a.   true
      b.   false

12.23 People apply stereotypes whenever they communicate with low awareness of others.

   * a.   true
      b.   false

12.24   Rarely, is language a major barrier to intercultural attempts.

    a. true
  * b. false

12.25   Anxiety can be a major stumbling block to intercultural communication.

  * a. true
    b. false

Short Essays

12.1   What is the role cultural variability plays in interpersonal communication? Answer in some detail.

12.2   "Every man is in certain respects (a) like all other men, (b) like some other men, (c) like no other man."—Kluckhon and Murray. Explain the meaning of this statement.

12.3   Define "culture shock." If there was a time when you experienced some degree of "culture shock," please explain the circumstances and the attendant feelings you went through.

12.4   As a male/female in this culture, how do you see your social role as at least somewhat gender-based? Be specific.

12.5   Cite at least two present-day generational differences which you are aware of which tend to create a rift between the "older" and the "younger" generations.

12.6   In a paragraph, explain how gender orientation has become such an issue in American society in recent years. What possible reasons have brought this about?

12.7   Give at least two specific examples of "genderlect."

12.8   In some detail, explain how mainland China would be considered a high-context culture.

12.9   Why does empathy need to be fostered as an important intercultural communication skill? Is it possible to be truly empathic with a person from a markedly different culture and belief system?

12.10   What is meant by the term "assumed similarity?" Cite an example. What was the result?

CHAPTER 13

MEDIA LITERACY AND INTERPERSONAL COMMUNICATION: THE TECHNOLOGICAL EMBRACE

CHAPTER SYNOPSIS

Mass media is pervasive in our daily lives. Whether the medium is radio, television, film, computers, magazines or newspapers, to name a few, this prevalence has an "everywhereness" quality to it. What impact do these mediated forms of communication—human communication assisted by technology—have on interpersonal relationships? In exploring such a question, we can develop an awareness and understanding of the process of mediated communication and its effects on us.

Interpersonal and mass communication are intertwined. All human relationships have been influenced by media innovations. Media serve a linking function that allows us to stay in communication with others though we are separated by great distances and time. Media also serve as a model for interpersonal behavior and relationships. Our relationships are both reflected and infected by the mass media.

The phrase "**interpersonal mediated communication**" refers to person-to-person interaction through the use of a technological device to send and receive messages. Some interpersonal situations require media for communication. Because of the development of technology, people must choose which medium of communication to use in any given context. Our choice of media has consequences that can reach into the very essence of our life.

The consequences or effects of media on our interpersonal lives have been explored by several communication scholars who have developed theories describing these effects. Five prominent theories are **social learning theory**, **dramatistic theory**, **rhetorical fantasy theory**, **script theory**, and **symbolic interaction theory**.

Because the media influence our perceptions of daily life, they have the potential to influence interaction in close personal relationships. The images we receive from our use of media provide us with a **media reality** that is often different from our personal experiences. Media images influence **self-identity** including **sex-role development**, **gender expectations**, and factors of **ethnicity**.

There are four important strategies in dealing with mediated forms of communication in our interpersonal relationships. The first is to develop our **media literacy** skills—an informed and critical understanding of the nature of the mass media, the techniques used by them, and the impact of these techniques. The second is to **make appropriate technology choices** for any particular interpersonal task. Thinking through what we want to accomplish through

142

communication can help us to make the correct choice of a communication medium. Third, **making informed choices about when and where to communicate** with someone is important. When is our ability to use technology to reach someone almost 24 hours a day becoming intrusive? Conscious awareness of such a question can help us form appropriate communication strategies with new technologies. The fourth strategy is to **think critically about media, values, and interpersonal communication**. Mass media contain values, values that promote certain life orientations and not others. To raise our ability to deal with mass media messages, the best strategy is to use our critical thinking skills. We need to examine media messages for what they really are—constructed media reality.

This millennium has brought an explosion of change and an onslaught of high technology that has affected relational development. The future will provide even faster communication technologies. The task will be to use them appropriately and not to be used by them. This is only possible though conscious, intelligent effort.

CHAPTER OUTLINE

I.   Prevalence of Media in Our Daily Life
        A.   Communication Technology and Interpersonal Relationships

II.   Why Discuss Media in a Book About Interpersonal Communication?

III.   The Connection Between Interpersonal and Mass Communication

IV.   The Role of Media in Interpersonal Communication
        A.   Reflect Our Relationships
        B.   Infect Our Relationships

V.   What is Interpersonal Mediated Communication?
        A.   The Difference Between Media and Mass Communication
        B.   Media as Extensions
        C.   Choosing Your Medium

VI.   Consequences of Mass Media on Interpersonal Communication
        A.   Theory of Kenneth Burke
        B.   Theory of Ernest Bormann
        C.   Theory of Kevin Durkin
        D.   Theory of Erving Goffman
        E.   Cone Effect
                1.   Perceived Media Reality
                2.   Constructed Media Reality

VII.   Media Images and Media Reality
        A.   Self Identity and the Media
        B.   Sex Role Development

VIII.   Interpersonal Media Images
        A.   Modeling Behaviors

IX.   Media Literacy Strategies and Critical Reasoning
        A.   Becoming Media Literate
        B.   Making Appropriate Technology Choices
        C.   Choices of Time and Place
        D.   Thinking Critically about Media, Values and Interpersonal Communication

X.   Interpersonal Communication, New Technologies and The Future

TEACHING OBJECTIVES

▸   To present the significance of media in interpersonal communication both as a linking mechanism and as a model for "a way of being."

▸   To explore the possible influences of mass media on relationships.

▸   To delineate models for understanding the role of media as secondary learning experiences that influence our beliefs, values, and relationships.

▸   To explain the notion of media literacy and critical thinking skills helpful in dealing with "constructed media realities."

▸   To speculate on the continuing influence of new media technologies on interpersonal relationships.

TOPICS FOR STUDENT JOURNAL ENTRIES OR ESSAY ASSIGNMENTS:

1.   Over a period of three days log your media exposure. What types of media confront you every day? How much of your time is spent in media related events?

2.   How do movies and television affect the way you relate to others? For example, do two of you watch together a lot as part of your ritual as a couple?

3.   Think of a media event which has affected you most; for example, the Challenger explosion, an assassination, etc. Over which medium did you find out about this event? TV? Radio? Newspaper? How did the particular medium affect the message? That is, would the

impact on you have been different if you would have experienced this event through a different medium?

4.   Watch a series of soap operas or talk to someone who watches soaps regularly. What message does this show portray about society? Is that message reality? How do these soaps particularly parallel or diverge from the current issues or concerns?

IN-CLASS ACTIVITIES FOR STUDENTS:

1.   In small groups discuss the media's role in portraying stereotypes. Does the media portray any stereotypes about women? Minorities? Men? Children? Families? Does the media reflect the culture's already existing stereotypes or form these stereotypes? Does media mirror or shape reality?

2.   Think of people you know who have been affected by media in their interpersonal relationships. Talk in small groups about how this constant media exposure affects their interpersonal communication. Have you ever been influenced in your relationships by something in the media? Does the media reflect or infect interpersonal communication?

3.   In 2-3 larger discussion groups, address how fathers are presently portrayed on television as often bumbling, offish and childish (e.g. "Married With Children" or "The Simpsons"). What negative effects do such portrayals have on the image and status of fathers in this culture?

4.   Watch 2-4 short video clips from movies (e.g. "Field of Dreams," "Wayne's World," "A River Runs Through It," "Robin Hood: Men in Tights.") Which depict both examples of masculinity and the lack of masculine traits?

As a class, discuss whether these film depictions seem "accurate," "fair" and/or stereotypical. Does the medium of film usually depict men in this society accurately or do most male roles seem "typecast" or like caricatures?

5.   In 2-3 large groups, discuss how the media distort presentations of gender. Be specific with examples. Allow 30 minutes for in-depth discussion and note-taking. After 30 minutes, have a spokesperson for each group summarize their group's findings and discussion highlights.

Later, as a class, discuss how, as media patrons, we can affect positive changes in media gender images.

6.   As a class, discuss how we can determine the appropriateness of time and place for technological communication in our personal relationships. (Is it ever appropriate to telephone someone at 3:00 in the morning? Is it intrusive to leave several messages per day on someone's home answering machine?)

145

7.   As a class, discuss why people seem to have an almost insatiable appetite for various communication devices. Is this use of technological devices more of a help or a hindrance? When is it a help? When is it a hindrance?

TEST QUESTIONS

Multiple Choice

13.1   The technological devices that are used for the purpose of mass communication are:

       a.   telephones.
 * b.   mass media.
       c.   intermedia.
       d.   natural media.
       e.   all of the above

13.2   Over the past few years, as scholars began to see communication as a developmental transaction, the _____ became the essential element that distinguished interpersonal communication from other forms.

       a.   the use of mass media
       b.   the physical presence of two communicators
 * c.   the quality and type of communication
       d.   all of the above
       e.   none of the above

13.3   "E-Mail" stands for:

 * a.   electronic mail.
       b.   second-class mail.
       c.   entertainment medium.
       d.   elaborated codes.
       e.   none of the above

13.4   Person-to-person interaction through the use of a technological device to send and receive messages is termed:

       a.   mass media.
 * b.   mediated communication.
       c.   symbolic interaction.
       d.   social interaction.
       e.   acoustical communication.

13.5   _____, a theorist, is credited with the terms "medium" and "media."

     a.   Gary Gumpert
     b.   Samuel Morse
     c.   Ernest Bormann
     d.   Kenneth Burke
* e.   Marshall McLuhan

13.6   If people are to understand the impact of media on their lives and relationships, they need to become _____.

     a.   informed
     b.   educated
* c.   media literate
     d.   empathic
     e.   sympathetic

13.7   The process of observing situations, individuals, or behaviors that affect personal attitudes and communicative behavior is termed:

     a.   spying.
     b.   observation.
     c.   studied evaluation.
* d.   social learning.
     e.   none of the above

13.8   The rhetorician who developed the concept of "rhetorical fantasies" is:

     a.   Socrates.
     b.   Plato.
     c.   Kevin Durkin.
* d.   Ernest Bormann.
     e.   Kenneth Burke.

13.9   To coordinate our relationships with others through the manipulation of symbols is termed:

     a.   symbolism.
* b.   symbolic interaction.
     c.   mediated reality.
     d.   social learning.
     e.   symbolic projection.

13.10 Whetmore's _____ looks at the relationship between real life and what we receive by way of various media.

   * a.   cone model effect
     b.   perceived reality
     c.   constructed reality
     d.   mediated message
     e.   media extension

13.11 A major influence on one's sense of self is:

     a.   direct experience.
     b.   indirect experience.
     c.   observations of symbolic behavior.
     d.   none of the above
   * e.   all of the above

13.12 The collection of behaviors that a given society deems more appropriate for members of one sex to the other is termed:

     a.   social roleplay.
   * b.   sex role.
     c.   gender label.
     d.   self-image.
     e.   behavior function.

13.13 Acts of affiliation such as expression of feelings, altruism and self-disclosure are termed:

     a.   intimate relationships.
     b.   fraternal relationships.
   * c.   prosocial messages.
     d.   antisocial messages.
     e.   social messages.

13.14 A strategy for dealing with mediated forms of communication is to:

     a.   become media literate.
     b.   make appropriate technology choices.
     c.   conscious awareness of time and place to communicate.
     d.   think critically about media, values, and interpersonal communication.
   * e.   all of the above

13.15   A media-literate perspective encourages one to:

  * a.   use media constructively and decode information.
    b.   model behavior appropriately.
    c.   choose the right television channels.
    d.   subscribe to T.V. Guide.
    e.   "reach out and touch someone."

13.16   According to Gumpert and Cathcart, "_____ have affected what we know, who we talk about, who talks to us, and who listens."

    a.   foreign cultures
  * b.   modern electronic media
    c.   international relations
    d.   radio and television
    e.   fax machines

13.17   A type of "natural" media is:

  * a.   sound.
    b.   common sense.
    c.   the brain.
    d.   waterways.
    e.   none of the above

13.18   Learning acquired from media images or characterizations is termed:

    a.   social education.
    b.   socialization.
    c.   imitation.
  * d.   social learning.
    e.   media propaganda.

13.19   A generalized representation that helps people understand the world is termed a:

    a.   play.
    b.   docudrama.
  * c.   script.
    d.   enactment.
    e.   performance.

13.20 People's perception of media reality is a highly selected process. This process begins when:

    a.   one is born.
    b.   one becomes literate.
    c.   one reaches the approximate age of 7 years—age of reason.
* d.   one chooses which medium to use and how closely to pay attention to it.
    e.   one becomes media literate.

13.21 One of the following is not a form of mass extensions:

    a.   radio
* b.   magazines
    c.   fax machines
    d.   computers
    e.   satellite

13.22 The term _____ is used to look at everyday human behaviors as a kind of drama.

    a.   scenario
* b.   dramatistic
    c.   symbolic interaction
    d.   daily script
    e.   none of the above

13.23 On a literal level, "scripts" provide clear-cut _____ for everyday life.

    a.   models
    b.   behaviors
    c.   ideas
    d.   roles
* e.   all of the above

13.24 CMR stands for:

* a.   constructed media reality.
    b.   communication medium reality.
    c.   constructed mediated realm.
    d.   communication mass retrospective.
    e.   clear media reliability.

13.25   Weaver and Wakshlag suggest that when direct experience is lacking or ambiguous, _____ is formed through lower-order influences such as television.

      a.   memory
  * b.   perception
      c.   modelling
      d.   experience
      e.   learning

True or False

13.1   Communication media have the ability to bring people together or to distance them from each other.

  * a.   true
      b.   false

13.2   According to the text's authors, the media in the past decade do not distance people from each other but actually links people together over great distances at the speed of light.

  * a.   true
      b.   false

13.3   It isn't so much what people talk about that is important in interpersonal communication; rather it is how they relate to each other that is significant.

      a.   true
  * b.   false

13.4   All human relationships have been influenced by media innovations.

  * a.   true
      b.   false

13.5   Interpersonal relationships are both reflected and infected by the mass media.

  * a.   true
      b.   false

13.6   A person's self-image and its development are media dependent.

  * a.   true
      b.   false

13.7   Essentially, the terms "mass media" and "mass communication" are synonymous.

    a.   true
*   b.   false

13.8   The telephone is an example of a mass media device.

    a.   true
*   b.   false

13.9   An example of a "media extension" is the human voice.

    a.   true
*   b.   false

13.10   Our choices of media have consequences that can reach into the very essence of our lives.

*   a.   true
    b.   false

13.11   For sociologist Erving Goffman, the self is determined by the roles people project in daily "staged" presentations.

*   a.   true
    b.   false

13.12   Secondary learning has a powerful influence on everyone and hence, on everyone's relationships.

*   a.   true
    b.   false

13.13   Sex role development begins in the womb.

    a.   true
*   b.   false

13.14   The messages of mass media are among the most controversial in human communication.

*   a.   true
    b.   false

13.15   In media advertising, a surprising 70% of females do voice-overs on commercials.

      a.   true
  * b.   false

13.16   One antisocial message often portrayed on T.V. presents fathers as inept when called on to help with their daughters' problems.

  * a.   true
      b.   false

13.17   According to research, even in situational comedies on American T.V., there is an underlying tone of hostility.

  * a.   true
      b.   false

13.18   Television is probably the most persuasive media tool in American homes.

  * a.   true
      b.   false

13.19   According to James Chesebro, there is not an actual "intimate relationship" between the television shows we view and the ways in which we communicate and govern our lives.

      a.   true
  * b.   false

13.20   Our U.S. culture could be accurately described as a television culture.

  * a.   true
      b.   false

13.21   Over the last fifteen years, research indicates that the media distort presentations of gender.

  * a.   true
      b.   false

13.22   Though the mediums of popular television and film, we learn what relationships are like.

      a.   true
  * b.   false

13.23   Because of television, many people tend to envision the typical black community as violent, dirty and dangerous.

   * a.   true
     b.   false

13.24   Media messages are basically mediated reality.

     a.   true
   * b.   false

13.25   For good or ill, people seem to have an insatiable appetite for communication devices.

   * a.   true
     b.   false

Short Essays

13.1   How does media impact your daily life? Be specific.

13.2   What are the differences between media and mass communication?

13.3   Do you feel you are media literate? Which media do you feel most comfortable with? Have you been taught to think critically about media or do you use it mainly as a pastime?

13.4   Discuss the concept of "mediated reality."

13.5   In your opinion, does the average American watch too much TV daily (surveys indicate an average of six hours)? What are some of the negative social effects of too much television viewing?

13.6   What are some of the positive effects of growing up in a television culture?

13.7   How do media serve as models for interpersonal behavior and relationships?

13.8   What are 4-5 prosocial messages you have derived from television viewing the past week? What are 4-5 antisocial messages you were exposed to? (Don't overlook the use of commercial messages.)

13.9   What are some examples (minimum of 4) of outstanding communicative behavior which you have viewed through the media (television, film) in the past month?

13.10   At some length, complete this statement:

By the year 2,050 A.D., interpersonal communication will have reached new levels. It will be an era when...

CHAPTER 14

COMMUNICATING IN SMALL GROUPS

CHAPTER SYNOPSIS

One of the most important practical communication skills is the ability to work with other people in small groups. This chapter focuses on describing a number of small groups and their various goals. Virtually all organizations utilize small groups either to enhance a feeling of belonging or to solve problems that inevitably arise in an institution.

Scholars in communication are divided about how small or large a group should be to properly function. Most suggest a number between five and fifteen, but this range is not carved in marble. Size depends on the task and the time a group has.

The chapter includes a description of four different groups—learning, social, encounter and problem solving—and delineates their purposes. Attention is paid to how small groups can be successful.

People join groups for a number of reasons, which range from socialization to practical problem solving. Many still believe the old adage that many heads are better than one. Ideally members of a small group will pool their collective expertise and use sound reasoning as they attempt to untangle problems.

While in theory, groups should be better at solving problems than an individual, sometimes a group approach can backfire. One well known example is Irving Janis" principle of "groupthink." Janis maintains that because of group pressures to conform, many fail to contribute their best thinking and as a consequence often produce failures rather than successes.

Part of the reason for groupthink relates to the stages a small group goes through. Tuckman has described typical phases as forming, storming, conforming and performing.

For example, groups that conflict on the idea level (storming) are often more productive than those who don't.

The leadership of a group is usually central to how well it functions and succeeds in attaining its goals. A brief review of leadership styles is presented to make this point. Most scholars agree that no one style of leadership should apply in all situations, but that a particular style might work better because of the members involved and the format chosen.

The chapter concludes with a description of how one group—President John Kennedy's cabinet—failed in their attempts to address Fidel Castro's takeover of Cuba. This in turn, produced the "Bay of Pigs" fiasco. The same group, however, learned from their mistakes and effected what many historians describes as one the greatest problem solving ventures of the twentieth century.

CHAPTER OUTLINE

I.   Definition of a small group

II.   How big should a group be?

III.   Various types of groups
    A.   Learning
    B.   Social
    C.   Encounter
    D.   Problem solving

IV.   Why become involved in these groups?
    A.   Social: people like them
    B.   Groups activities
    C.   Attraction to group goals
    D.   Find meaning and identity
    E.   Association
    F.   Problem solving
        1.   Pool collective expertise
        2.   Use best thinking of the group members

V.   Groupthink
    A.   Symptoms
    B.   Established norms are difficult to deviate from that norm
    C.   Lack of critical analysis to problem solving
    D.   Diverse groups less susceptible

VI.   Phases in group development
    A.   Four most common (Tuckman's model)
        1.   Forming
        2.   Storming

3. Norming
   a. Explicit
   b. Implicit
4. Performing

VII. Roles
   A. Group task roles
   B. Group maintenance roles

VIII. Group problem solving that works
   A. The importance of the leader in successful group problem solving
      1. Leader's style: brief review of four kinds
      2. Approaches to leadership
         a. Functional approach
         b. Transformation approach
         c. Situational approach
      3. Difference between designated and emergent leaders
   B. Sound critical thinking
      1. Logical validity
      2. Supporting evidence
      3. Effective process: Dewey's Reflective Thinking Model

IX. Apply all the steps above to the Cuban missile crisis

TEACHING OBJECTIVES

▸ To emphasize the difference between various types of small groups

▸ Describe the phases a group goes through in making a decision or solving a problem

▸ To explain how leadership impacts a group

▸ Demonstrate how critical thinking skills can help a group function effectively

TOPICS FOR STUDENT JOURNAL ENTRIES OR ESSAY ASSIGNMENTS:

1. Describe one effective and one ineffective meeting you have attended. What made them effective or ineffective? What communication aspects contributed to the effectiveness of ineffectiveness of the meeting?

2. Based on an examination of recent world or national events, which groups seem to be offering well thought out decisions to problems they're facing? Which groups seem to be drifting toward "groupthink"?

3.   Some people have described encounter groups as "touchie, feelie." Do you agree with this assessment? If not, how can an encounter group help individuals who have major relational problems?

4.   Assume you're in a problem solving group of twelve people. Early in the deliberations, it becomes obvious to you that the designated leader Herb is far from being the most influential in the group. In fact, Nancy demonstrates the most leadership skills. What would you do about this situation? Would you let is happen or say something you think would solve the problem and help the group better achieve its goals?

IN-CLASS ACTIVITIES FOR STUDENTS:

1.   Spilt the class into four groups. Each group will perform a skit demonstrating one of the four various types of groups: learning, social, encounter, and problem solving.

2.   In the past year have you been involved in any groups where groupthink existed? What did you do to override the groupthink?

3.   In groups, each person will take turns as the leader, by carrying out one of the ideal leadership responsibilities: providing the members with a plan, reducing tension when it occurs, keeping the group on task, and promoting critical thinking skills.

TEST QUESTIONS

Multiple Choice

14.1   The size of groups should

     a.   be limited to three
     b.   more than five
* c.   depend on the task and the time a group has
     d.   have twelve members
     e.   none of the above

14.2   Which of the following is not one of the various learning groups?

     a.   Learning
     b.   Encounter
* c.   Reacting
     d.   Problem-solving
     e.   Social

14.3   In the _____ group, people come together to pool their collective expertise and to use their critical thinking skills solve a problem outside the domain of any one individual.

    * a.   Problem-solving
      b.   Social
      c.   Reacting
      d.   Learning
      e.   Encounter

14.4   What is one of the five reasons why people join groups?

      a.   They like to sit around and gossip.
    * b.   People's need to find meaning and identity.
      c.   conforming
      d.   They dislike of the groups' goals.
      e.   None of the above.

14.5   Which of the following, is a reason for joining a group with the goal of getting a specific politician elected?

      a.   people's needs to find meaning and identity
      b.   interpersonal attraction to members of the group
      c.   conforming
    * d.   attraction to group goals
      e.   all of the above

14.6   When selecting members of a group, which is the least important factor?

      a.   experience
      b.   intelligence
      c.   knowledgeable
      d.   cooperative
    * e.   born leader

14.7   _____ is a drive consensus by groups with little attention to critical thinking.

      a.   Forming
      b.   Norming
    * c.   Groupthink
      d.   Brainstorming
      e.   none of the above

14.8   Groupthink can lead individuals to:

    a.   form unique decisions
    b.   establish various viewpoints
*   c.   abandon their usual set of values or moral codes
    d.   all of the above
    e.   none of the above

14.9   Which of the following do not dictate the best kind of leader?

*   a.   personal wealth
    b.   experience as a leader
    c.   ability to use critical thinking
    d.   openness to different points of view
    e.   none of the above

14.10   Which of the following is not one of Tuckman's stages of group dynamics?

    a.   forming
*   b.   re-forming
    c.   storming
    d.   norming
    e.   performing

14.11   _____ is one of the most important stages because members can experience conflict on at least two levels.

    a.   Forming
    b.   Re-forming
*   c.   Storming
    d.   Norming
    e.   Performing

14.12   Which of the following is a false statement about norms?

    a.   they are habits a group adopts
    b.   open discussion of goals, roles, and group tasks is undertaken
    c.   students raising their hands waiting fort the teacher to call upon them before making a response
    d.   once established, it is difficult to go against norms
*   e.   all norms are productive

14.13 _____ refer to expectations and patterns of behavior people exhibit within a group.

      a.   Goals
* b.   Roles
      c.   Performing
      d.   Explicit norms
      e.   none of the above

14.14 Typical group task roles are which of the following?

      a.   initiator-contributor
      b.   information seeker
      c.   opinion seeker
      d.   information giver
* e.   none of the above

14.15 _____ help the interpersonal relationships between group members and contribute to group cohesiveness.

      a.   Group task roles
      b.   Individual roles
      c.   Group maintenance roles
* d.   none of the above

14.16 Which of the following is/are an example(s) of individual roles?

      a.   encourager
      b.   compromiser
      c.   clown
      d.   procedural technician
* e.   all of the above

14.17 Which is not one of the four leadership styles that leaders commonly display?

      a.   autocratic
      b.   bureaucratic
      c.   persuasive
      d.   participative
* e.   dictatorship

14.18 Which of the following best portrays one of the various types of groups that enjoy self-enrichment?

     a.   playing chess
     b.   taking out the trash
     c.   talking about a new best seller
  * d.   both a and c
     e.   none of the above

14.19 Which one of the following is one of the most crucial roles for effective problem solving?

     a.   overpowering others in the group
     b.   groupthink
     c.   raising your hand
  * d.   leadership
     e.   all of the above

14.20 In which of the following steps of reflective thinking do participants suggest possible solutions without analyzing each one in detail?

     a.   establish criteria
     b.   groupthink
     c.   discussing the symptoms of a problem
  * d.   brainstorming
     e.   finding causes

14.21 John F. Kennedy and his cabinet members were successful in dealing with the Cuban Missile Crisis because:

     a.   they had better intelligence information than the Soviets.
     b.   they effectively used critical thinking skills.
     c.   they were not afraid to argue ideas.
     d.   they learned from their mistakes.
  * e.   more than two of the above

True or False

14.1 Unfortunately, small groups often make worse decisions than individuals do.

  * a.   true
     b.   false

14.2   An autocratic master sergeant would be a good match for young army recruits.

   * a.   true
     b.   false

14.3   An autocratic master sergeant would be a good match for a collection of older, experienced faculty members.

     a.   true
   * b.   false

14.4   The situational approach means leaders must balance their style according to the situational needs of the group.

   * a.   true
     b.   false

14.5   Often a group over fifteen will follow parliamentary procedure based on Robert's Rules of Order to make sure all parties are heard.

   * a.   true
     b.   false

14.6   A learning group is sometimes called an educational or focus group.

   * a.   true
     b.   false

14.7   Focus groups are designed to learn people's ideas, values, and opinions on an issue.

   * a.   true
     b.   false

14.8   The encounter group is also known as the personal growth group.

   * a.   true
     b.   false

14.9   The encounter group was designed to help a company solve a problem of sagging sales.

     a.   true
   * b.   false

14.10 People may join groups because they have an interpersonal attraction to members of the group.

    * a.   true
      b.   false

14.11 Some people may join groups because they are considered prestigious.

    * a.   true
      b.   false

14.12 Small groups in an organization are formed on the assumption that many heads are better than one.

    * a.   true
      b.   false

14.13 If a group has a leader who uses a persuasive style, it will always succeed.

      a.   true
    * b.   false

14.14 The situational approach demands leaders who have a particular charisma that encourages loyalty.

      a.   true
    * b.   false

14.15 The third step in reflective thinking is to find the best solution.

      a.   true
    * b.   false

14.16 The functional approach assumes there are particular things a leader does to be a leader.

    * a.   true
      b.   false

Short Essays

14.1 Discuss the leadership style you prefer to work with and why. Try to avoid superficial responses.

14.2 What are the differences and similarities between an encounter and a problem-solving group? What is the purpose of each purpose of each kind of group?

14.3 List and discuss four suggestions for conducting successful meetings in small groups.

14.4 Explain two different situations using implicit and explicit norms.

CHAPTER **15**

PUBLIC SPEAKING SKILLS

CHAPTER SYNOPSIS

The art of public speaking can be traced back to the ancient Greeks and Romans. We still owe a great debt to Aristotle and Cicero who provided some of the first treatises about effective public speaking. Both stressed the importance of a wide background since skilled speakers project more than a pleasant voice, but have to have something worthwhile to say. The five Canons— originally attributed to Cicero—can still provide a useful framework for students giving public speeches in class.

In the 21st century, good speeches resemble more polished conversation than the bombastic oratory of pre-television days. Speeches these days are receiver oriented in the sense that an orator is conscious of the audience and their attitudes.

Stagefright—or podium panic--is a problem for everyone who delivers a talk, but such a problem can be overcome with some proven methods. One of the most helpful is the use of the "energizer effect" that occurs when a speaker is nervous, has an audience but has prepared carefully. All three of these elements coalesce to make the speaker's mind even more alert than if she or he wasn't nervous.

The chapter includes some specific ways for students to organize and deliver their presentations along with three outlines of speeches students might give during the term. The five elements of delivery help students appreciate the importance of their own delivery. Especially important are projection and rate. Speakers who project with energy find themselves less nervous than those who don't, plus their audience will be more interested in their talks. A slower rate allows presenters to think ahead to better decide on what words they want to use.

The chapter contains some tips on utilizing such non-verbal items as what to wear during a speech, the importance of posture, gestures and audio-visual aids.

Different types of speeches receive treatment. These include extemporaneous, impromptu, memorized, demonstration, informative, persuasive and speeches to entertain. The chapter concludes with a list of criteria teachers can use to evaluate speeches.

CHAPTER OUTLINE

I.   Background
      A.   The Ancients
            1.   Aristotle
            2.   The Five Canons
      B.   Contemporary Approach

II.   Dealing With Speechfright
      A.   Why It Occurs
            1.   Physiological Reasons
            2.   Psychological Reasons
      B.   Good news about nervousness
            1.   The Energizer Effect
            2.   Acting Confident

III. Preparation
      A.   Picking A Topic
      B.   Organizing Material
      C.   Research Strategies
      D.   Blending Research Into the Speech

IV.   Transitions and Internal Summaries

V.   Memory

VI.   Association
      A.   Imagination
      B.   Repetition
      C.   Using Vivid Imaging

VII. Long And Short Term Preparation

VIII. Delivering the Speech
      A.   Projection
      B.   Rate
      C.   Vocal Quality
      D.   Inflection
      E.   Enunciation

IX.	Non-verbal Elements Of Public Speaking
	A.	What To Wear
	B.	Posture And Gestures
	C.	Audio/visual Aids
	D.	Different Kinds Of Speeches

X.	Speech Evaluation

TEACHING OBJECTIVES

▸	To help students see speechfright as something positive.

▸	To provide some practical ways for students to organize speeches.

▸	To focus on effective ways to deliver public speeches.

▸	To help students use audio/visual aids in making presentations.

TOPICS FOR STUDENT JOURNAL ENTRIES OR ESSAY ASSIGNMENTS:

1.	Remember a time when you were nervous about giving a speech in public. How did you cope with your nerves? Did the nervousness interfere with the speech during delivery? Did you feel like a success or a failure afterwards?

2.	How have you gone about organizing a speech? Did you skip making an outline or some other form of putting the speech together? If you did prepare an outline, how in-depth was it? Was the depth of the outline determined by how much you knew about the topic?

3.	When you are delivering your speech in public, do you speak louder and slower than usual? Do those two approaches alleviate some of the nervousness you may be feeling?

IN-CLASS ACTIVITIES FOR STUDENTS:

1.	Get together with three or four other students and discuss the most difficult speech you've ever had to give. Why was it so challenging? Then talk about the best talk you've delivered. Why was it successful? Can you apply what made it work to a speech you have coming up in class?

2.	Try a short "fanatic speech" in which you assign an unpopular topic to students. Stand behind each student and let him or her get out the opening two sentences before raising your arms—a signal that the audience should start booing and hissing. The speaker should keep talking and use more projection than usual to be heard over the noise of the audience. When the short speech is finished, ask the student if nervousness decreased. It should because the greater projection helps reduce the butterflies.

3.   Watch video speeches of great speakers and then discuss why they are so skilled. Great speakers on video include Martin Luther King, Barbara Jordan, Ronald Reagan, Mario Cuomo, Winston Churchill, Margaret Thatcher and Franklin Delano Roosevelt.

4.   If feasible, have students give one speech that includes PowerPoint slides. Before they speak, discuss the benefits and liabilities of PowerPoint. For example, while PowerPoint can provide sparkle to any presentation, overuse can take the audience's attention away from the speaker and influence them to focus on the slides.

5.   Videotape one or two speeches throughout the semester. After having students watch themselves on tape, ask them first what they LIKE about their performance. Most of the time, speakers will start with what they didn't like. Then ask them what they think they might do to improve for the next time.

TEST QUESTIONS

Multiple Choice

15.1   The person who is known as one of the greatest orators of the Roman era is:

  a.   Aristotle.
  b.   Quintillian.
 * c.   Cicero.
  d.   Gorgias.
  e.   Julius Caesar.

15.2   The five canons of speech are:

 * a.   a pattern of preparing and delivering a speech.
  b.   a musical group in the fifties.
  c.   an invention of the ancient Greeks.
  d.   an invention of the British in the 19th century.
  e.   more than two of the above.

15.3   Most people feel nervous feel nervous before delivering a speech because:

  a.   they fear failure.
  b.   they can feel their heart beating faster.
  c.   lack of control.
  d.   a vivid remembrance of a time they failed giving a speech.
 * e.   more than one of the above.

15.4   The first two elements of the energizer effect are nervousness and an audience. The third one is:

      a.   you have audio visual aids.
  * b.   you prepare using the vivid imaging method.
      c.   you are enthusiastic about the topic.
      d.   you project your voice.
      e.   you exercise an hour before your speech.

15.5   Disposition is which of the following aspects of the Five Canons:

      a.   preparation.
  * b.   organization.
      c.   style.
      d.   memory.
      e.   delivery.

15.6   Research sources can include:

      a.   the university or college library.
      b.   faculty members.
      c.   the internet.
      d.   video tapes.
  * e.   all of the above.

15.7   Vivid imagery includes:

      a.   the imagination of key points in a speech.
      b.   forming pictures in your mind.
      c.   using your power of reason.
      d.   bringing an actual picture to your audience.
  * e.   more than one of the above.

15.8   Articulation also means:

      a.   vocal quality.
      b.   projection.
      c.   style.
  * d.   enunciation.
      e.   more than two of the above.

15.9   A speech that involves a minute or less of preparation is

      a.   extemporaneous.
   * b.   impromptu.
      c.   demonstration.
      d.   a report on a single event.
      e.   a speech to persuade.

15.10   A way of reading an audiences' possible attitudes is called

      a.   extrapolation
      b.   attitude adjustment scale.
      c.   semantic differential.
      d.   electron.
      e.   none of the above.

15.11   Statistics are one form of evidence. Other kinds of evidence include:

      a.   expert testimony.
      b.   factual.
      c.   contrived.
      d.   hearsay
   * e.   two of the above

15.12   Unfairly attacking a speaker's character is the fallacy of

      a.   red herring.
      b.   slippery slope.
      c.   false conclusion.
   * d.   ad hominem.
      e.   narrow casting.

15.13   Analyzing an audience fits under what category of speech evaluation?

      a.   organization
      b.   delivery
   * c.   invention
      d.   style
      e.   none of the above

True or False

15.1   Public speaking is also an interpersonal skill.

    * a.   true
      b.   false

15.2   Contemporary speeches are basically polished conversations a speaker uses to connect to an audience.

    * a.   true
      b.   false

15.3   Most stress is brought on by lack of control.

    * a.   true
      b.   false

15.4   Picking a topic is almost always the easiest part of preparing a speech.

      a.   true
    * b.   false

15.5   Plagiarism refers to trying to pass off somebody else's work as your own.

    * a.   true
      b.   false

15.6   Internet was not available until 1991.

    * a.   true
      b.   false

15.7   A speaker should prepare an introduction before moving on to the preparation of the body of the speech.

      a.   true
    * b.   false

15.8   An internal summary is one effective way of making a transition between major points in a talk.

    * a.   true
      b.   false

15.9   Humor should never be used in a formal presentation.

      a.   true
  * b.   false

15.10   In most speeches, a speaker is better off using a memorized manuscript over an outline.

      a.   true
  * b.   false

15.11   When preparing a speech, one should never practice in front of a mirror.

      a.   true
  * b.   false

15.12   Projection is a combination of volume and vocal energy.

  * a.   true
      b.   false

15.13   Vocal quality is the same as vocal inflection.

      a.   true
  * b.   false

15.14   Is it highly distracting for a speaker to hold on to a lectern during a presentation.

      a.   true
  * b.   false

15.15   A speaker should ideally have an aid visible only when making a specific point about the object of demonstration.

  * a.   true
      b.   false

15.16   Audio-visual aids are discipline specific.

  * a.   true
      b.   false

15.17　A demonstration speech usually requires props and other visual aids to demonstrate a particular technique.

　　　* a.　true
　　　　b.　false

15.18　Ethos describes the speaker's competence and rapport with an audience.

　　　* a.　true
　　　　b.　false

15.19　A humorous speech is probably the easiest to give since everyone is having a good time.

　　　　a.　true
　　　* b.　false

15.20　Audio-visual aids should rarely be used when giving a persuasive speech.

　　　　a.　true
　　　* b.　false

Short Essays

15.1　How can a liberal arts education help make someone become a better speaker?

15.2　Even though the Five Canons go back to ancient times, why might they help you do a better job of organizing a talk?

15.3　Why is it more effective to write an outline for your speech rather than "just let it flow naturally"?

15.4　Please explain why the "vivid image" method of remembering will help a speaker maintain better eye contact with an audience?

15.5　For the introduction, why is it better NOT to announce your topic in the opening sentence? What should come first?

15.6　Why is it so important to analyze carefully the predominant attitudes of your audience?

15.7　In evaluating a speech—yours or someone else's—what is the difference between content and delivery. Why are both important?